Thomson Nelson

Report
Writing

Second Edition

MW00682884

Thomson Nelson Guide to

Report

Writing

Second Edition

Lawrence Gulston
Sir Sandford Fleming College

THOMSON

NELSON

stralia   Canada   Mexico   Singapore   Spain   United Kingdom   United States

THOMSON
NELSON

Thomson Nelson Guide to Report Writing, Second Edition
by Lawrence Gulston

Associate Vice President, Editorial Director:
Evelyn Veitch

Editor-in-Chief, Higher Education:
Anne Williams

Acquisitions Editor:
Bram Sepers

Marketing Manager:
Shelley Collacutt Miller

Developmental Editor:
Theresa Fitzgerald

Content Production Manager:
Tannys Williams

Production Service:
Gex Publishing Services

Copy Editor:
Eliza Marciniak

Proofreader:
Gex Publishing Services

Indexer:
Gex Publishing Services

Production Coordinator:
Ferial Suleman

Design Director:
Ken Phipps

Interior Design:
Gex Publishing Services

Cover Design:
Katherine Strain

Cover Image:
Comstock Images

Compositor:
GEX Publishing Services

Printer:
Transcontinental

COPYRIGHT © 2008, 2004 by Nelson, a division of Thomson Canada Limited.

Printed and bound in Canada
1 2 3 4 10 09 08 07

For more information contact Nelson, 1120 Birchmount Road, Toronto, Ontario, M1K 5G4. Or you can visit our Internet site at http://www.nelson.com

Statistics Canada Information is used with the permission of Statistics Canada. Users are forbidden to copy this material and/or redisseniate the data, in an original or modified form, for commerical purposes, without the expressed permissions of Statistic Canada. Information on the availability of the wide range of data from Statistics Canada can be obtained from Statistic Canada's Regional Offices, its World Wide Website at <http://www.statcan.ca> and its toll-free access number 1-800-263-1136

ALL RIGHTS RESERVED. No part of this work covered by the copyright herein may be reproduced, transcribed, or used in any form or by any means—graphic, electronic, or mechanical, including photocopying, recording, taping, Web distribution, or information storage and retrieval systems—without the written permission of the publisher.

For permission to use material from this text or product, submit a request online at www.thomsonrights.com

Every effort has been made to trace ownership of all copyrighted material and to secure permission from copyright holders. In the event of any question arising as to the use of any material, we will be pleased to make the necessary corrections in future printings.

Library and Archives Canada Cataloguing in Publication

Gulston, Lawrence
   Thomson Nelson guide to report writing / Lawrence Gulston.—2nd ed.

First edition published under title: Nelson guide to report writing.
ISBN 13: 978-0-17-644241-5

   1. Report writing. 2. Technical writing. I. Title.

T11.G86 2007   808'.0666
C2007-900796-1

CONTENTS

PREFACE

The *Thomson Nelson Guide to Report Writing,* Second Edition, is designed to be a brief, useful guide to current report format and writing practice for scientific and technical writers at college and in the workplace. It can be used as a course text, lab manual, or writer's guide and resource as he or she develops a piece of scientific or technical writing of any length.

The *Thomson Nelson Guide* directs students to deal with the central issues of writing a report: research and organization of information; writing in a clear, readable style; formatting report pages; dividing the text into sections; writing appropriate report elements; integrating graphic presentations to support text descriptions; and documenting secondary sources of information.

The student writer typically consults a book like this after attempting a report assignment and finding trouble. Before writing a first draft of your report, skim this book. It will speed up the writing process by reducing the amount of revision necessary. Starting the first draft of a report with the right elements in the right place, the right graphics in the right place, and all the sources cited and listed in the correct form means less work and better results.

This text is a guide only. Each topic discussed is an overview of a complex subject, from documentation systems to styles of rhetoric to grammar and sentence syntax. It is hoped that the inclusion of frequent specific examples of scientific and technical reporting will help students and professional writers to produce documents that communicate effectively. For those requiring greater detail or a more theoretical approach, textbooks are available in composition and technical writing.

This book is a general guide to report writing for students and must be supplemented by professors who have more specific requirements for their students' writing projects. It is important for faculty to set out format expectations for written work in clearly stated assignments.

The report format in this guide is primarily for scientific and technical reporting. It includes an abstract, which is used in place of the letter or memo of transmittal and the executive summary. General business reports differ in significant ways from scientific and technical reports, and they vary considerably in design and in content.

At the suggestion of reviewers, this book has been organized to reflect the writing process, rather than the order of elements in a report. Students must consciously follow a sound methodology in constructing a technical or scientific document in order to achieve an efficient, effective communication. Their tendency to focus on details of format inhibits their ability to focus on the overall goals of technical communication and appropriate methods of achieving those ends. We do present information about report format as a reference for students with specific questions or issues to resolve. However, they must always see this problem-solving activity in the larger context of the writing process.

The section on documentation describes the three major formats currently in use in scientific and technical reporting. Writers and professors will be able to choose the format that best suits their needs. Examples of each format include forms for electronic sources currently in widespread use such as web pages, CD ROM, and e-mail. The same examples are repeated in each format for comparison.

The Appendix includes tutorials for creating special report formats using Microsoft Word XP™ word processing software. These include formats for reference lists, mathematical equations, and wrapping text around graphic figures.

Acknowledgements

I wish to acknowledge the support, encouragement, and patience of the Thomson Nelson publishing team: Anne Williams, Bram Sepers, Beth Lariviere, and Tannys Williams. I would also be remiss if I did not acknowledge the support of the faculty, staff, and students at Sir Sandford Fleming College, without whom the first edition would not have been written. Finally, I wish to dedicate this book to my children: Jennifer, Sandy, Brian, and Anthony.

Chapter

Report Research and Organization

1

Overview: This chapter addresses the most important part of report writing: identifying your audience and purpose. It also discusses team-based report writing, effective research methods, organizational processes, and report planning.

1.1 AUDIENCE AND PURPOSE

Have you ever found yourself sitting in front of a blank computer screen when you have to write a report, wondering what to write about, or how the document is supposed to look? Did you know that there is a simple answer to those questions?

Everything you need to know about content and format of your report can be learned by examining the needs of your intended audience and your purpose in writing. Thinking about these things before you write will save you time and produce a better report. "In my report, should I tell the boss about the late delivery on Thursday afternoon?" "No, it didn't put the project schedule behind, and that's what matters to the boss who has to read my report."

We often write things down to satisfy personal needs and goals, for example in a diary or an e-mail to a friend. However, the words we use sometimes do not signal all of our intended meaning. They are incomplete expressions that readers have to fill in from their own knowledge base or from their knowledge of our personality. When we reshape our words into complete meanings in order to satisfy the needs and goals of others, we begin to communicate efficiently and effectively. Good communication gives both personal satisfaction and professional success.

The reshaping process, however, takes work. A scientist or a technician can expect to spend 20 percent of his or her working week creating written documents. That's one working day out of five.

The Goals of Technical Writing

The purpose of scientific and technical writing is to present your readers with accurate, complete, and current information about your work, in a way that is appropriate to their needs. The conventional types of scientific and technical reports are designed to meet the needs of readers in specific workplace situations—for example, progress reports that update managers on the progress of company projects and proposals that set out proposed company projects in detail and persuade the reader to approve the work.

Scientific and technical data are often complex. Writing about them requires you to organize the data and the accompanying concepts into a coherent narrative that is accessible and can be understood by your readers.

The Readers of Scientific and Technical Writing

The primary audience for your report will be the person or group who will read your document and take responsibility for its contents, such as following up on recommended actions. The secondary audience will be persons or groups interested in its contents, such as technicians doing similar work, company executives monitoring progress, and so on.

The better you know your audience, the better you will be able to know what they what to read about and in what form. Personal communication with your audience is the best way of gathering complete information about that audience's needs. Such communication can take make forms, from asking your boss which field results to include in the monthly report to distributing a survey among park visitors to determine the topics that they would find most interesting to read about in a park newspaper or outdoor presentation.

Types of Audiences

Readers of scientific and technical literature can be grouped according to similar interests as follows:

- *Experts* are well educated and look in reports for scientific and technical data, usually presented in graphic form, and for interpretation of experimental results.

- *Technicians* look for solutions to practical problems.
- *Managers* look for information about how time and money were spent and for cost-effective solutions to technical problems.
- *Operators of equipment* look for clear, well-illustrated instructions.
- The *general public* looks for simplified explanations of processes and products.

The Purpose of Technical Writing

Most scientific and technical reports are written to convey specific information to specific readers. The word *report* itself comes from two Latin words meaning "to carry back." The most important part of your job, once the lab or field work is done, will be to "carry back" the results to people in your organization who need it.

As you become proficient in writing reports, you will find yourself better able to influence workplace decisions. For example, supervisors may ask you to follow up on well-researched and organized reports with recommendations for action. Effective reports have a persuasive purpose, in addition to their basic function of informing the reader.

Other purposes of scientific and technical writing include the following:

- to uncover facts
- to separate facts from opinion
- to make valid and convincing conclusions
- to record and discuss findings from field and lab work
- to provide facts that support an informed opinion
- to move from general data, such as that found in encyclopedias, to specific information, such as that found in reports, field studies, textbooks, and monographs.

State your purposes clearly in the introduction to your report. Use action verbs: "to investigate," "to develop," "to compare and recommend," and so on. Your reader wants to know why your report was written. Writing down your purpose helps clarify your work goals and assists in deciding what to include in the report.

A report written at the end of your lab or field investigations brings back to your workplace and your supervisor information that is useful, often vital, to the company's operation. Presenting this information clearly and logically is the key to your career in science and technology.

1.2 WRITING IN TEAMS

The Purpose of Team Writing

Writing in teams, or collaborative writing, is common in the workplace because it has the following advantages:

- *Expertise.* Scientific and technical projects require a wider range of skills and expertise to reach a goal successfully than a single writer can provide.
- *Feedback.* A writing team can provide a variety of viewpoints on the developing text in terms of its style and its content. In most cases, this feedback helps produce a report that better communicates with its intended audience.
- *Networking.* Scientists and technicians find that working on writing projects in teams is less lonely and offers important opportunities to network and share information. It improves communication among employees and provides an introduction to corporate culture for new employees.

However, writing in teams has the following disadvantages:

- *Time.* Collaboration means communication, which takes time. Writing teams require more time to produce documents than individual writers do.
- *Conformity.* Team members often work harder at cooperating with each other than at asking difficult questions of each other in order to produce a better document.
- *Workloads.* In most teams, some members do more work than others. Some team members remain unmotivated to contribute work of good quality because they have been given less to do, because they perceive they have too much to do, or because they have experienced conflicts with other team members.

Team writing will not go away because of these potential problems. In the contemporary workplace, the ability to work with others has become as important as technical competence. A wise strategy for a college student is to learn better interpersonal and communications skills to complement scientific and technical skills.

Approaches to Team Writing

Two different approaches to team writing are commonly used by workplace writing teams. The first is co-authoring. In teams of two or three people, co-authoring means that each team member takes responsibility for organizing and writing a section of the text, with regular feedback from the other team members. The second is consulting. In larger teams, consulting means that a writer or a writing team takes responsibility for developing the plan of the report, coordinating the expert input of the other team members, and editing the text.

Members of successful writing teams are aware of the interpersonal dimensions of the team and willing to take personal responsibility for their actions. They treat the other team members as they themselves wish to be treated. They respect the others' strengths, seeking out their ideas and special skills and finding ways to use them in the writing project. They insist on excellence in their own work and in the project's final written documents but without becoming perfectionists over unimportant details.

A good team writer does the following:

- conducts efficient, diplomatic team meetings
- listens to others and contributes ideas
- asks good questions
- uses technology effectively to communicate.

Building the Team

The following tasks are carried out by highly successful report-writing teams.

- *Elect a leader.* One team member must take responsibility for communicating with team members and monitoring progress.
- *Divide the work equally.* First, brainstorm the topic independently, then bring your notes to a team meeting. Identify the main areas that need to be researched. Assign equal amounts of research to each member of the team and monitor progress. Write down the agreed division of work and make each other accountable for it. In a student writing team, all members should be writers and editors to hone their skills and learn from each other.
- *Make a schedule.* List completion dates for each major step in the work of research and writing.

- *Meet regularly.* Review team progress and adjust goals and deadlines as needed. Take notes to ensure that deadlines are being met and work is equally distributed.

- When drafts of sections are complete, copy and distribute them to team members for *peer review*. When a complete draft of the report is ready, have a team meeting to look at inconsistencies of style and content. Review the final draft of the report twice.

Reviewing Each Other's Work

When reviewing each others' work, use the following sound strategies:

- *Set writing goals and standards.* Criticism based on personal preferences for writing style and format is not helpful. Discuss and agree on your writing goals before you begin the writing process. You may wish to set a style sheet with key points or use a standard guide such as this textbook.
- *Include positive as well as negative comments.* Applaud team members for their achievements. Praise forms the basis for trust and positive change when criticism is necessary.
- *Make criticisms specific, not vague.* To improve the report, team members must know clearly what you have perceived as a problem and know what to do about it. Include viable solutions with your criticism.
- *Do not rewrite the draft,* tempting though this may be. Help each other to be better writers by leaving team members with helpful, encouraging comments to act upon.

Editing

Team leaders must take control of planning and scheduling the editing work, keeping records of drafts, monitoring progress, communicating with team members, and distributing manuscripts. The editing process should follow the same sequence as the writing process, focusing on content, language, and format.

- *Content.* Read through the content to ensure that it is complete and accurate. If field or laboratory test results are part of the report, consult your notes to make sure that the data in the final draft is correct.

Check that the content is coherent and follows a logical sequence. Ensure that no significant parts are missing, that there is no irrelevant material, and that the subject matter is given a balanced treatment.

- *Language.* Edit for correctness. Errors in spelling, grammar, punctuation, and usage are serious barriers to understanding and affect the team's credibility. Edit for good style. A report should be concise, so reduce wordy constructions to simple, direct language. Look for good transitional words and phrases between sentences and paragraphs; these provide the context essential to meaning. In technical reports, use appropriate terminology when describing scientific and technical content.

- *Formatting.* The design of a report is important. It provides accessibility to the reader and impresses corporate clients with its clean look and order of elements. Check the form and order of report elements from title page to appendix. Be sure they are complete, correct in form, and correctly ordered. Take special care with the documentation system; it is your reader's guide to your sources of information. Manuscript form requires double spacing. Graphic elements must be presented in a format large enough to be seen clearly, and each must carry an appropriate table or figure number, title, and, if borrowed from an external source, a citation of source in the same system that is used throughout the report text. Finally, decide on the appropriate physical presentation for the report, such as spiral binding.

1.3 RESEARCH

Gathering Information

Before you write, you must have something to write about. Usually, finding a topic is not a problem in the workplace. Circumstances will make it clear what you have to write about. Your focus, then, must be getting all the information about the situation and selecting details carefully for your chosen reader or readers. There are two main types of information sources: primary and secondary. You should be familiar with the distinction and know how to effectively use information from both kinds of sources.

Primary Sources

Your training and proficiency in lab and field procedures will be reflected in the notes you take. Recording accurate data on a clipboard or personal data assistant (PDA) means careful attention to scientific detail and technical processes. A good technician double-checks details and figures for accuracy, since accurate detail is the lifeblood of technical reporting. A scientist must record every detail of a procedure, even the mistakes.

Record experimental information in a notebook with bound pages, and open each entry with the date and time. Use the same format for similar kinds of experimental procedures. Record everything that happens, but avoid explaining anything. It is easy to jump to conclusions, but you should remember that the proper place for interpreting your data is in the final report. Do not confuse inferences and judgments with facts.

Use standard format on data sheets or readouts from instrument faces for most field and lab recording. Use your notebook to record extra information not included on standard forms and instrumentation, such as weather conditions, unusual variations in meter readings, and so on. Write down observations as soon as possible after they happen. Such journal entries will be essential to accurate interpretation of the data later.

These lab and field data, combined with the overview of the project from your personal notes, are your primary sources of information and form the basis of the text of your report, as well as the source material for its tables and figures. Good notes will help make a good report.

Secondary Sources

The Purpose of Using Secondary Sources

In most reporting situations, you will be asked to interpret the data you have collected. In order to draw valid inferences and support your conclusions with authority, it is necessary to read scientific and technical material written by others in professional journals, technical bulletins, conference papers, and the like, and then to compare these printed findings with your own data.

Secondary sources are also widely scanned by technical staff for solutions to technical problems. If an engineering technologist is faced with unacceptably high current drains in a new electromechanical device being designed, he or she will look for ways to reduce the current drain while maintaining optimum output performance by researching similar designs in technical literature.

Finding Secondary Sources

Materials found through library and web research are the most common sources of scientific and technical information for college and workplace reports. Company and department files also supply timely, specific information.

Prioritize your research by looking in the most likely places first for the information you and your reader need.

A library is organized for easy access of materials and contains information in print. Most North American libraries use the Library of Congress classification, although some local libraries still use the Dewey Decimal system. Know the system in your library to locate useful materials quickly, and learn to use reference tools, such as subject indexes and specialized dictionaries and directories. Information in print has been reviewed and edited during the publishing process, and it has been selected by library staff to meet readers' needs, which makes library resources generally more reliable, accurate, and thorough than any other kind of secondary sources.

The Internet is not a library. It is a dynamic system of billions of documents and digital files, each with a very short average life span. These publicly accessible documents and files can be found using search engines such as Google, directories such as Yahoo, and metasearch engines such as Metacrawler. All can be located by the Uniform Resource Locator (URL) system, often called the web address. When searching for documents, learn how to select keywords carefully, observing spelling conventions and paying attention to shades of meaning. A small change in spelling can give you a big change in search results. Many private companies operate their own private Internet-accessible intranet sites, which contain files that cannot be found by search engine software and are reserved for corporate use. These corporate pages have helpful, company-specific information for employees to use in their report writing.

Most wise web researchers look for lists of links compiled by experts in their subject areas. Experts in various scientific and technical fields search the Internet for web sites with current, authoritative, complete information and put up pages of hyperlinks to these resources; usually, each link is accompanied by a summary and assessment of the information on the linked site. Since so much information on the web is incomplete or inaccurate, such lists of good resources prepared by knowledgeable people can be quite useful, if they are current. Always check pages for the date of last update.

The Internet can also help during the drafting phase of writing, offering a wide range of online dictionaries, thesauri, encyclopedias, and writing labs that deal with matters of report style and format. It can also be a source of digital image files to support scientific and technical descriptions in your text. Be sure to ask for permission before using any borrowed images.

Using Secondary Sources

Before taking notes from secondary sources, write down all the details about your source of information that are required by your documentation system; you will need these later for citations and reference list entries in your report.

As you read your source information, take notes by paraphrasing the key ideas and information. Paraphrases are your own personal combinations of keywords and phrases from the original—what you select in your reading as important information and write down as a collection of points.

Beware of the photocopier and the cut-and-paste function on your computer. They make it easy to ignore the essential process of reading text and understanding ideas. Is that hard work? Yes! Admittedly, it is easier to highlight some phrases on a photocopy or to paste a section of text from a web page to a draft in your word processor. But doing that won't help you understand the original, and your final report will still sound like somebody else's. If you don't cite your source of information, the disaster is complete: you've committed plagiarism.

Select brief quotations carefully. Use quotations for specific examples of general ideas and for exact statements of general principles. Limit direct quotations to one or two sentences wherever possible, and do not use more than two or three direct quotation examples per report.

1.4 ORGANIZATION

The Importance of Organizing

Finish your research when your project has ended and no data are left to report or when time runs out before the report has to be written. Leave yourself enough time before the report deadline to organize the information, write and revise the drafts, and set up the document in its final format.

Before you can start writing, organize your research. Organization is the key to readability in your report. Use ideas to organize facts. Learn common patterns of organization—comparison, more-to-less-important pattern, classification and division, cause and effect, problem/solution, and so on—and let them guide your report plan.

Look for ideas in your notes or in discussions with other professionals. If you have a visual imagination, try sketching your ideas. Try to answer the journalistic questions: who, when, where, how, and why. Your own knowledge and experience will suggest relationships within your research information. To make sense to your reader, your facts must be connected to each other and form a pattern.

Outlining

Outlining is the process of grouping information together into logical units and making descriptive headings for those units. Planning before you write saves you time and gives your report the quality of structure, a logical progression of facts that helps your reader understand the material faster and better.

A formal outline is an information hierarchy. It consists of descriptive headings that you will place in the report to inform your reader of the location and the type of information presented. When you write the first draft, the headings will guide you as you develop the text in each topic area that you have to cover.

Good thinking skills are important in constructing a formal outline because the hierarchy of headings depends on logical connections. There are many practical ways to improve your thinking skills. The CoRT Thinking Skills© developed by Edward de Bono are a good example. Taking a college-level course in thinking skills is another. A good technical writer is also a good thinker, working through technical data and ideas methodically and logically according to sound thinking principles. The quality of your thinking will be reflected in the structure of headings in a report outline.

Outlining takes practice. Fortunately, you will have many opportunities in college and in the workplace to practise the art, starting with routine e-mails and moving on to longer forms of writing. Do not miss an opportunity to organize a piece of writing, no matter how small.

The following is a simple, four-step method for working with your research notes to produce a formal outline consisting of headings.

1. Collect your research notes and read them through until you know them completely and the big picture begins to emerge.

2. Divide your notes into two, three, or four major areas of concern. Give each of those areas a name. Use the keywords from your research notes to form the descriptive title. Do not worry about

details here. If something does not fit into your main categories, set it aside. Consider it later; it will usually fit into a more completely developed outline, or it will be irrelevant to your report and can be eliminated.

3. Look at each major report topic in turn. Divide each into two, three, or four subtopic areas and give each a more specific topic heading. A topic heading consists of a noun and its modifiers. Continue this process, dividing this second level of organization into a third level with headings and so on until you find you can write several paragraphs under each heading. Then stop.

4. Check your outline for logic and correct format. Give the outline a working title, using the keywords in your main headings, and check your outline for a logical sequence of headings and for errors, such as faulty coordination, faulty subordination, or faulty parallelism. Coordination means placing equally important headings at the same level of organization. Subordination means placing information in the category where it logically belongs. Parallelism means using the same keywords in descriptive headings for similar kinds of information to signal the similarity clearly to your reader and make the comparison of your data easier. Format your outline in a standard form, using either the traditional numbering system or the decimal numbering system for the headings. Indent each level of organization about five spaces. The format for the formal outline allows you to see more clearly, through numbering and indentation, the relationship of the ideas expressed by the headings. This makes a final check for errors easier.

Outlining requires taking the time to become familiar with the research information for your report and to work through the development of a hierarchy of descriptive headings. However, it saves time in the long run by speeding up the process of drafting the report. It also helps produce a better organized product. Documents covering scientific and technical topics need to have a simple, clear plan of organization. That plan must also be available to the reader so that he or she can find specific topics to meet specific needs in a timely manner. For this reason, your outline will form the basis of your table of contents.

I. Introduction
   A. Purpose and Scope
   B. Review of Literature
   C. Study Area
   D. Background

II. Maya Writing
   A. Sources of Texts
      1) The Codices
      2) The Stelae
      3) Monuments
      4) Ceramics

   B. Forms of Maya Writing
      1) Letters
      2) Numbers
      3) Phonemes

III. The History of Maya Epigraphy
   A. Tatiana Proskouriakoff
   B. Linda Schele
   C. David Stuart and the New Epigraphy

IV. Glyphs of Three Major Cities
   A. Tikal
   B. Copan
   C. Palenque

V. Conclusions
   A. Altering Maya History
   B. Importance for Modern Maya
   C. Importance for Archaeology

Box 1.1: Sample Outline for Report on Mayan Epigraphy

Common Patterns of Organization

Organizing your information is your first and most important step in connecting your report with your audience. Learn to recognize common patterns of organization, such as those discussed below, in published reports and use them in your own writing. Your reader will also recognize these patterns and thereby understand the content better and faster.

Use patterns of organization flexibly. They will guide your thinking as you look for relationship in the data contained in your research notes and help you establish a logical order. These patterns are not rigid rules or formulated categories, such as a questionnaire or a lab sheet. Rather, they are general patterns of thinking that form the basis of much scientific thought. As such, they give a recognizable structure to your writing and provide the basis for drawing logical conclusions from your data.

Modify and combine these patterns to suit your report. If you need to explain one aspect in greater detail than the others, do so. Make sure that your descriptive headings reflect this amount of detail by showing more subheadings in that area. Combine patterns in longer reports by using different patterns to organize different material within major and minor sections of the report. For example, in a report comparing three or four computer systems, set up criteria for comparing them first, listing and describing the criteria in the more-to-less-important pattern.

Some patterns of organization are so simple that they need no explanation. Time and space are two of these. Technical procedures, for example, are best described step-by-step in sequence in which they happen in real time. The same is true of technical processes, such as signal processing in a radio receiver, which begins with the radio frequency input. When organizing spatial information derived from field work, move consistently north to south or east to west, describing the features of each area in turn. The following sections discuss several other commonly used patterns of organization.

Comparison

Comparison is common in reports that present scientific and technical data for two or more possible choices and end with recommending one of them. For example, feasibility studies for new landfill sites require environmental assessment of several possible locations and make recommendations regarding the best choice. The basic pattern of the report is comparing Site A with Site B and so on.

In individual paragraphs and sentences explaining scientific and technical processes and principles, this pattern allows the writer to expand the reader's understanding from something familiar to something unfamiliar. For example, to explain a zebra to a child who has never seen one, the writer can begin by comparing the zebra to something familiar, such as a horse, to give an idea of size and conformation. Then the writer can add what is different about the zebra, such as its black-and-white stripes. This pattern of development is sometimes called the "given–new" strategy. Show your reader the similarities between the familiar and the unfamiliar process or principle you are explaining, then proceed to show the differences.

Establishing Criteria

Establish criteria for your comparison when using this pattern for the major sections of the report. Criteria are the needs and standards used to compare data. If criteria are not applied consistently to the data, the comparison and the conclusions drawn from it will be invalid. For example, describing one computer's motherboard and fast bus speeds and then describing another computer's hard drive and Ethernet card does not provide the basis for a valid comparison.

Whole-by-Whole and Part-by-Part Comparisons

Most writers faced with comparing complex scientific and technical data will have to choose between two possible methods of doing so: whole-by-whole and part-by-part. It is better to understand the choice and make it knowledgeably. Many writers struggle to express complex detail in writing because they have not grasped the underlying pattern of development.

In whole-by-whole comparison, the writer describes each option that is being considered in the report completely and thoroughly. The description of each option is organized into categories that correspond to the criteria established at the beginning of the report.

Whole-by-whole comparisons work best when the information is relatively simple and straightforward, without complex detail.

In part-by-part comparison, the criteria for selection become the major organizing categories. The writer describes each criterion before describing how each option in turn fulfills that criterion.

II. Comparison of Systems
    A. Dell
        1. Software
        2. Memory
        3. Disk Storage
        4. Cost
    B. IBM
        1. Software
        2. Memory
        3. Disk Storage
        4. Cost

Box 1.2: Whole-by-Whole Comparison of Computer Systems

Part-by-part comparisons work best when information is complex. Use this pattern when both the criteria and the options that you are exploring require more detailed description and explanation of scientific and technical principles and processes.

Either of these patterns of comparison may be combined in a report with the more-to-less-important pattern. If this applies to your situation, prioritize the criteria for comparison and present them to the reader in more-to-less-important order.

More-to-Less-Important Pattern

Most readers of scientific and technical reports want to know what is important. They rely on your judgment about the factual information and the concepts presented in your report.

The more-to-less-important pattern presents the main ideas first. Look at the points you want to make in a section of your report. Are some more important than others? Can you say why?

If the answer to these questions is "yes," begin with an explanation of the reasons for your set of priorities. Then organize your points in a list from the most important to the least important.

The more-to-less-important pattern requires that you evaluate your data objectively and describe your priorities or your company's priorities fairly. The scientific reader, for example, expects to read the most important research findings first. The executive reader expects to read answers to the most urgent questions first.

The more-to-less-important pattern is particularly useful in persuasive writing, such as one finds in a business proposal. When summarizing the reasons for a particular action or the benefits of choosing your company to do the work, place your descriptions of the most important reasons or benefits first.

Use vertical lists with numbers or bullets to summarize the main points in a more-to-less-important list. Make descriptive heading for your points and use the headings to show the pattern of organization.

II. Comparison of Systems
    A. Software
        1. Dell
        2. IBM
    B. Memory
        1. Dell
        2. IBM
    C. Disk Storage
        1. Dell
        2. IBM
    D. Cost
        1. Dell
        2. IBM

Box 1.3: Part-by-Part Comparison of Computer Systems

II. Reasons for Choosing My College
    A. Excellent Reputation
    B. Lower Fees and Living Costs
    C. Semi-rural Location

Box 1.4: The More-to Less-Important Pattern

Classification and Division

Classification is the process of putting items with similar characteristics into the same category. Categories help us organize and understand the world. In a broad sense, classification is what scientists and engineers do when they gather information about how the world works; they group phenomena, everything from the natural world to building materials, into useful categories. The thinking process that involves looking first at the details and then classifying them into larger, descriptive categories is called induction, or inductive reasoning.

Categories can contain subcategories. This is because some ideas are large and inclusive of many observable details, while other ideas are smaller and include less detail, depending on finer and finer distinctions within a basic category.

Division is the process of dividing a general subject into specific component parts. The thinking process that involves looking first at the main idea or theme and then dividing it into smaller, descriptive categories is called deduction, or deductive reasoning.

Use division for descriptions of mechanisms, instruments, and processes. For example, in the description of an instrument, divide the instrument into a number of discrete component parts. Describe each part by dividing it into its component parts and explaining the form and function of each.

To better understand the difference between induction and deduction, think of describing trees and a forest. If you start with the trees instead of the forest, you are classifying, or using induction. You will note that the white pine and the red pine are both pines, that is, they share basic characteristics, along with the jack pine and the Scots pine. The same process of looking at the data will add categories such as firs and spruces. Eventually, you may see the white oak and the red oak, giving you oaks to add to maples, birches, and poplars. At the end of the process, you will see that the pines, firs, and spruces share characteristics different from those of the oaks, maples, birches, and poplars, yielding the two largest categories of trees: softwoods and hardwoods.

If you start with the forest as a whole, you are dividing, or using deduction. You can divide the forest into the softwoods and hardwoods and then break these up into the various categories of both types. The process ends when you are describing individual tree species, the smallest data set.

The Abstraction Ladder
A visual way of seeing classification and division is the abstraction ladder (see Figure 1.1). Imagine a household stepladder. At the narrow top of the ladder is the main idea, or theme of your report. At the broad base of the ladder is

your data in all its diversity and individuality. When you move up the ladder from the particulars to the general ideas, you are classifying; when you move down the ladder from the general to the particular, you are dividing.

Developing a Classification System

Here are some points to keep in mind as you develop a classification system for your report.

- Avoid overlapping categories in your classification system wherever possible. For example, if you were to use "water snakes" and "poisonous snakes" as categories to describe reptiles, snakes such as the deadly water moccasin would fit into both categories. Work through

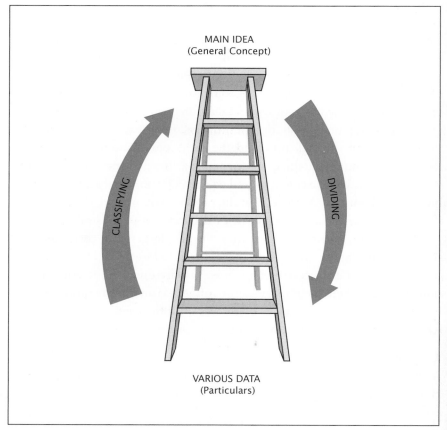

Figure 1.1: Abstraction Ladder

the logic of categories in your outline to ensure that characteristics forming the basis of classification remain consistent throughout the outline and at each level of the outline. In some areas of science and technology, overlap cannot be avoided because definitions of characteristics are not precise. In these cases, keep overlap to a minimum to provide your reader with a clear, logical classification system.

• Remember to write for your audience and purpose. A scientific audience will prefer induction and expect you to present the data as you found it before reading your analysis and any general conclusions you may wish to draw. A business audience will prefer deduction and expect you to state the main points of your report first before providing the technical details in logical categories. Check the characteristics on which your categories are based. Will your audience find this distinction useful? For example, categories of canoes based on fine distinctions between regular and ultralight Kevlar™ construction will suit knowledgeable canoeists but may not matter at all to the cottager who wants only an occasional paddle down the lake.

• Write a good outline first. Outlining requires grouping similar items together into categories that can be identified with clear, descriptive headings. It also requires that the categories be listed in logical sequences and divided into logical units. This grouping process is the essence of using classification and division to organize your report. A good outline is an information hierarchy with consistent, balanced categories. It includes all the categories that describe the main topic, leaving out nothing of significance. Writing a good outline requires knowing all your research information in detail, having good judgment about which data sets belong together, and being able to express the organizing characteristic for each category in a simple topic heading. As we have already discussed, the benefits of putting this effort into an outline are numerous: the report is easier to draft, the quality of the final product is bound to be higher, and your reader will have an easier time of understanding your information and finding the specific topics that he or she needs to read about.

• Use only one characteristic at a time to classify your data. For example, if you wish to classify the coins in your collection, you may select denomination as the first organizing characteristic. After you have gathered all the $2, $1, and $0.25 pieces into piles, you may then sort the remaining coins into silver, copper, and alloy coin categories. Any change in organizing characteristics would make the whole classification system invalid and confusing—and not useful when attempting to identify and access individual pieces in the collection.

Cause and Effect

The cause-and-effect pattern works in two reporting situations. The first is a report discussion that seeks to predict the outcome or effect of a given action or set of actions, the causes; for example, "If we raise the voltage to the oscillator, what effect will this have on the intermediate-amplifier output?" or "If the government passes regulations against using polyethylene liners in landfill sites, what alternative materials can be used to seal leachate from the water table?" The second is a report discussion that describes an unpredicted phenomenon, or effect, and seeks possible causes; for example, "When we installed bluebird boxes in this area, why did the squirrel population increase?" or "When we added reinforcement to this end of the structure, why did the other end shift slightly?"

Examining cause-and-effect relationships in science and technology can be problematic. Environmental factors are often complex and vague, difficult to identify and isolate experimentally. It is therefore important to describe such causal connections carefully in your report, with attention to as broad a range of detail as possible. Reason through your information logically, using conventional and accepted forms of analysis.

Organize your report by presenting your research findings first and then discussing the possible causes and effects.

- First, describe your research goals, along with the reasons for them (if relevant) and the methodology you used to investigate causes and effects.
- Describe your results in terms of either cause-and-effect or effect-and-cause. For example, "The following are the alternatives to polyethylene liners that our team considered viable" or "The following are the test results from the team's investigation of the structure after it shifted." It is not always easy to know when you have all the facts. Your own training, experience, and common sense are usually the best guide. When you are satisfied that you have considered all factors, it is time to write the report.

- Analyze the data in a discussion section. Share your reasoning with the reader. How you add up the factual information will determine how persuasive your argument is. Examine your assumptions carefully and discuss them with your reader. Show also the analytical techniques you used, making sure they are appropriate to your audience. For example, detailed mathematical analysis of data will not be useful to a manager who wants to read only your conclusions and recommendations.
- If required by the situation, end with a section of recommendations. As with the choice of data to present and the methods of analysis, your choice of recommendations will depend on your own training, experience, and common sense.

Errors in Logic

Errors in thinking can easily creep into your scientific and technical work, so be sure to always include a double-check step as you prepare your report. The beauty of writing about work is the opportunity it gives you to think about what you are doing and see it again objectively, to ask yourself whether errors were made in collecting and analyzing data or in developing solutions.

Errors in a scientific or technical discussion of causes fall into two categories. Assuming a causal relationship where none exists is one kind of error; assuming no causal relationship where in fact one exists is the other kind. Writing things down allows you to do a double check of your assumptions and catch such errors.

A scientific or technical report uses the language of statistical probabilities. An investigation rarely proves a case beyond any doubt; it can only reduce the probability of error to an acceptable level and increase confidence in test results.

Thinking about causes and effects is a large undertaking. A practical approach in your writing is to revise your report drafts looking for specific errors in logical thinking that technical writers often make in discussions of causes and effects. The most common types of errors are described below.

Appeal to the Person (Ad Hominem)

Avoid focusing on personalities or personal characteristics. In Latin, *ad hominem* means "to the man/person." If your analysis focuses on the character of a person or group, not the quality of their reasoning, you are diverting attention from the facts and analysis. Your report should have an *ad rem* (Latin for "to the thing") focus, emphasizing the evidence.

This error can occur in your writing when you examine evidence or discuss alternatives that you do not like. Personal bias can appear as name calling, prejudice against various groups in society, or associating the alternative with unpopular social groups.

Circular Reasoning (Begging the Question)

Don't assume the truth of your statement; prove it. Consider the following example: "The Sasquatch printer is the best laser printer because it is better than the others." Such a statement simply restates in the second part the assertion made in the first part. We have many different words to say the same idea. A circular statement adds nothing to the argument and does not prove the initial assertion to be true.

Watch for any statements in your report that take the form of "X is good because it [some specific example of good]," where "good" can take many forms, for example, "The Flashy microchip is valuable because it processes data faster."

Sampling Errors

Many environmental phenomena can be causes or effects, and they can influence a cause-and-effect relationship between other factors. Therefore, it is essential to gather as much information as possible under the constraints of time and resources to carry out your investigations.

Choosing a sample large enough and composed in a way that lets you draw reliable conclusions is a matter of expertise in statistical methods.

We are all guilty of drawing general conclusions based on fragmentary evidence. Consider, for example, the following statement: "The Sasquatch is an unreliable car because my friend's Sasquatch is unreliable." Making an assertion of this kind is sometimes called "jumping to conclusions" or, as a geologist friend once called it, "extrapolating on the basis of one sample."

The Error of "Post Hoc Ergo Propter Hoc"

In Latin, *post hoc ergo propter hoc* means "after the thing, therefore because of the thing." In this error of logic, we assume that the second of two observed events caused the first. In truth, if Event A comes before Event B, it doesn't necessarily cause Event B, although there may be a scientific correlation. In your own lab and field work, you observe many events during the course of testing. When doing causal analysis of the results, look for causes in the order of events but see beyond to the specific mechanisms that prove a causal relationship.

In order to prove that one event or circumstance caused another, you must show that the first event happened before the second. You must also prove a cause-and-effect relationship between the two events. The mistake in logic occurs when you prove that Event A came before Event B and then just assume that A caused B without showing specifically how that occurred; for example, "Bluebird boxes cause squirrel populations to increase because we counted more squirrels after we put up the boxes."

Problem/Solution

The problem/solution pattern of report organization comes from the reporting situation itself. For example, your boss may have encountered a problem that affects your department or company and has asked you to investigate the problem and report on it, including options for solving the problem.

This pattern of organization follows the natural pattern of work. The sequence of sections in your report is the same as the sequence of steps that you took to confirm, investigate, and analyze the problem, finishing with descriptions of possible solutions.

This pattern also applies to business opportunities. Your boss may not have a "problem" as such. He or she may see an opportunity in changing current engineering or technical practices or in developing a new product. Improving current systems is an ongoing process in business and industry. The sequence of work and of sections in your report will take the problem/solution format.

Use the following pattern of topics for your report:

- Describe the circumstances of the report: the problem and your mandate to investigate it or the opportunity to improve existing products or systems.
- Confirm the problem. Your initial investigation will be an environmental scan, looking at the circumstances surrounding the problem or opportunity and determining whether or not this problem or opportunity exists and, if so, what its potential impact on your company might be.
- Describe the methods you used to investigate the problem.
- Describe the results of your investigation. Use tables, graphs, and other visuals where appropriate to show this information. Summarize your results in a vertical list organized from most to least important results.
- Describe options for solving the problem or taking advantage of the opportunity. List them with the most important option, from your point of view, first.

- If the reporting situation requires you to make recommendations, write a separate section at the end indicating which option you recommend and reviewing the data and the reasoning you used to make the choice.

When investigating and reporting on a problem, remember that your reader, usually your immediate supervisor, will want to make his or her own choice of actions in the matter. To meet this need, set out clear, specific, well organized information regarding the nature of the problem, the methods used to investigate it, the results of your investigation, and the likely options for solving the problem. Your own training and experience are the best guides again as to how to investigate the problem and which data to report.

Scientific and technical researchers know that the choice of research methods determines the kind of information that you can develop. Therefore, it is important in the problem/solution report to describe your reasons for choosing a particular method or set of methods for investigating the problem. Such a description permits better analysis of the results and boosts the reader's confidence in workable solutions when you describe them.

Do not overstate the solution. It is natural, as you become involved in the investigation, to develop a sense of which option is the best solution to the problem. This natural tendency can result in promoting one solution over another in various ways or in promising results from one course of action beyond what is reasonable or even possible. Be aware of your own biases in this regard. Check your report drafts when you revise and edit for clues that you have overstated the solution, such as statements that use emotional language and sections that describe some solutions in greater detail than the others.

Write an overview in your introduction. Your reader will need a summary of the problem, the methodology, and the proposed solutions. Format your report with descriptive headings and provide the contents and illustrations elements to guide your reader to specific sections of your report.

1.5 PLANNING YOUR REPORT

As you develop an outline for the content of your report, make two important lists: a list of the report elements you will need to meet your reader's format and access needs and a list of the report graphics you will need to support your text descriptions and provide information in standard format.

The front matter consists of the pages before the body of the report, including the title page and table of contents. The back matter, which comes after the report body includes the reference list and the appendix. These elements provide key information about the report, summarizing and helping the reader locate specific topics and information within the text.

Plan front and back matter to meet your reader's needs and expectations. Then, as you write the first drafts of the text, you can identify information from the text that you will need to include elsewhere, such as page numbers required by a table of contents or reference entries required by citations of secondary sources in the text.

Plan your report graphics with a preliminary list. As you read your notes, look for field or lab data that must be summarized in your report in the form of a table, graph, or chart. These are conventional methods of reporting data; they are compact in form and easier for your reader to interpret and understand.

Also look for diagrams, charts, maps, or photos in your research materials that provide clear, convenient explanations of scientific or technical processes or instrumentation. Scientific and technological structures, theories, and processes must be visualized to be understood clearly. A good technical report balances good writing with good graphic communication. As with all borrowed information, cite your sources thoroughly.

CHECKLIST FOR REPORT RESEARCH AND ORGANIZATION

During your research and organization stage of report writing, be sure that you have done the following:

- Identified the primary audience, type of reader, and any secondary audience.
- Identified the purpose and stated it clearly in one or two sentences.
- If working as part of a team, established your role on the team, attended regular team meetings, identified team strengths and weakness, avoided pitfalls of team writing, and used effective team communication.
- Gathered all primary and secondary research materials.
- Made a summary notes of key points and recorded information about secondary sources.
- Written an outline, with the information organized into a hierarchy, with clear topic headings, correct subordination, and logical sequence of topics.
- Checked the outline for patterns of organization.
- Checked the outline for errors of logic.
- Checked the outline for formatting errors.
- Checked the outline for faulty coordination, subordination, or parallelism.
- Made a list of required front and back matter as well as graphics.

C h a p t e r

The Report-Writing Process

2

Overview: This chapter looks at how you actually write a report—the process of setting down your thoughts and ideas as words and pictures—and discusses the principal activities in writing: drafting, revising, and editing.

2.1 OVERVIEW OF STEPS IN WRITING A REPORT

Before we examine in detail how to write a successful report, familiarize yourself with the following main steps in the process, so that you can plan effective use of your writing time.

1. *Gather all available research materials.* Primary sources may include your field or lab testing results, notes and journals, and e-mails sent during the project. Secondary sources may include print materials from libraries, electronic files, and company documents.

2. *Plan before you write.* Use a formal outline to create a logical, hierarchical sequence of descriptive headings for your report, based on your research notes. This plan will speed up your writing, keep your report organized, and provide your reader with descriptive topic headings needed for easy access to your information and ideas.

3. *Draft the main points of the body.* Write down your headings and paragraphs of description under each one. Use your research notes to develop complete, accurate descriptions of the material, focusing on keywords and phrases. Use your outline to get them in the right order under logical, descriptive headings.

4. *Write your concluding sections.* These will include a summary of the most important points and an analysis or reflection on them. If your audience and purpose require it, add a section of recommendations.

5. *Add graphic elements.* Choose tables and figures to add essential information and visualization to your main text. Illustrations are essential to good scientific and technical reporting. Design them to communicate complete, accurate information and to support comments and inferences drawn in the text. Integrate them fully with your text by including appropriate numbers, titles, labels, and textual references. Include graphics not essential to your discussion as appendices.

6. *Write your introduction.* The introduction sets the reader's expectations by explaining the plan and purpose of the report. Describe the reasons for writing the report and outline the logical order of headings that you have chosen for your report. Include all information your reader needs to understand the content of the report, such as a theory of operation or a map of the field study area.

7. *Finally, write the report elements.* Be sure you have the ones your reader needs. For example, if you have presented lab test results summarized as tables, you will need a list of illustrations. Assemble the information for each element and write it in the conventional format. As you place the elements in the report, check that each has the correct information and format and that each is placed in the correct order.

2.2 CREATING YOUR TEXT

Create the text of your report in three steps: drafting, revising, and editing.

1. *Drafting* means translating your research notes into words, sentences, and paragraphs to express the essential content. Many student writers think that the text is complete after the first draft. Professional writers know that this is only the beginning.

2. *Revising* is the process of altering the content of your report. Adding, omitting, and reordering your content is the most important step

in making contact with your reader and communicating the right information. Revising ensures that all the material useful to your reader is covered and that all appropriate descriptions of scientific and technical principles and practices are included.

3. *Editing* is the process of correcting your text—its style, its expression, its grammar, and its spelling. Correct English is universal English, understood by everyone with a fundamental grasp of the language. Precise technique is essential in a science lab to produce accurate, reliable test results; precise English is essential in a report to produce a document that communicates data and concepts accurately and reliably to the widest possible audience.

Let us now turn to a detailed explanation of each of these three steps, starting with the drafting stage.

2.3 DRAFTING

As you translate your research notes into words, focus on straightforward, clear descriptions of field or lab procedures and technical instrumentation. Professors and professionals working in your field appreciate being able to read about your work in simple, clear, descriptive terms. Your descriptions of current techniques and innovations will be essential to their business.

Keep in mind, however, that few people can create clear, simple texts the first time they express themselves in written words. Most writers find it difficult to choose from among many possible ways to express an idea. Many writers are afraid to fail, afraid to find that their own written descriptions are confusing and full of mistakes, and afraid to rewrite a report section several times, trying out different words and phrases to capture a difficult concept. Many also worry about spelling, grammar, and usage at this early writing stage, instead of focusing on essential information and leaving such matters to the end of the writing process.

Starting to Write

Start with the easy ideas and information. For primary research, describe your methods and results. Use the keywords in your notes that express important data and essential ideas. Weave them into your own sentences and paragraphs. For secondary research, organize your information in the order of your outline headings.

Focus on your outline and your research notes in order to create clear, direct descriptions. Your outline is an invaluable tool. It is your guarantee of an organized presentation of information.

As you compose, follow the logical sequence of headings in the outline. Write each heading and read the research material that applies to that topic. Then write down your own version of that information, using the keywords and phrases from your research notes to express the central concepts. Build your sentences around these words and phrases, paying special attention to topic sentences in paragraphs. Keep each paragraph short and simple. Break complex processes into small steps and describe each of them in a single, brief paragraph with a strong topic sentence. Use bulleted or numbered lists for all lists of more than three items, such as steps in a procedure, equipment or materials needed, and so on.

Draft quickly. Do not pause to rewrite sections of your text or to correct mistakes. Look at your notes, not the words appearing on the computer monitor. Trust the writing process. If a section proves hard to write, skip it and go on. You can return later with fresh expressions of the essential ideas.

Your first draft will give structure to your document, but not its final form. Do not try to make it perfect the first time. Very few professional writers can produce a near-perfect draft from scratch, considering all aspects of the text at once. The most effective method of writing is to leave revising and editing to later drafts. Allocate time in your work schedule to revise and edit your text so that it will be accurate and correct.

Take breaks as you write drafts. Writers take regular breaks from the job of writing. However, keep in mind that if you stop at the end of a section, you will have to overcome inertia the next time you sit at the word processor—that is, you will have to think through the issues of the next section of text in order to get started again. For this reason, it is better to stop in the middle of a paragraph or section. When you stop in the middle, you can start writing again more easily next time because you will know immediately how to end your paragraph or section. Ideas will flow.

Type with your eyes on your notes, not on the computer monitor. Ignore typing mistakes on your display and focus on your information. This method results in better content and is also more efficient, allowing you to type the first draft straight through in less time than you would need if you were to constantly stop.

Using a Word Processor

Most professionals write using computers with one or more word processing applications and usually with access to a printer. These technologies affect both writing habits and the products of the writing process. This section looks at the word processor and describes how to take advantage of its power and avoid some of its pitfalls.

- The speed and power of word processing software benefit the scientific and technical writer in many ways.
- Word processing software is fast and accurate.
- A word processor can highlight language and formatting errors in your text.
- Modern word processing software has advanced formatting features that allow you to place scientific and technical data in graphic form on the same page as the text. Your reader then can visualize and interpret your ideas faster and more completely.
- The computer allows you to find information from a variety of sources, such as the Internet, e-mail messages, digital databases, scanners, and digital cameras.
- You can store your developing text files on your computer or other data-storing device in convenient forms, and you can then make neat, professional-looking printouts on a printer.

However, computer technology is not without its burdens when it comes to writing. The speed of the computer can cause writers to draft, revise, and edit too hastily without taking the necessary time to reflect on content, style, and format. When putting words together to express yourself, slowness is a virtue.

The computer, with its capacity for instant communication and entertainment, can also shift a writer's attention away from the content of documents and important ways to connect with the reader, such as providing illuminating examples or adding a map to clarify spatial relationships. Good writing requires mental focus. The computer's capacity for multitasking can distract a writer. One of the best ways to minimize such distractions is to turn off text messaging, e-mail, and other software.

Finally, the variety of features in word processing software requires a writer to spend considerable time learning effective ways of using the software.

Ease of use, in turn, can lead an unwary writer to adopt lazy typing and editing habits.

Writing Scientific and Technical Descriptions

Most of your writing will be descriptive. Your goal will be to describe objectively and in detail the steps taken in field and lab work and the measured observations of results.

Learn to look for exact quantities and measurements and write them into your text. For example, a statement such as "The emitter current on the power transistor was very large" tells the professional and technical reader little useful information. In contrast, "The emitter current on the IC-12 NPN-type power transistor peaked at 250 mA when a bias voltage of 5 mV was applied to the collector" tells the reader a great deal more that is useful.

Keep your paragraphs short. A single paragraph covering an entire page is much too long. Write short paragraphs about smaller, more specific aspects of each topic. Introduce each paragraph with a strong topic sentence that states clearly the type of information that you have described in that paragraph.

Using Secondary Sources

The best way to use your secondary research material is to paraphrase it—that is, put the facts and ideas into your own language. Read your sources carefully and understand the content before trying to write it down. Do not attempt to replace key technical and scientific terms such as "photosynthesis" or "motherboard." They have no simpler equivalents that mean the same thing. Instead, focus on your sentences. Make sure that the sentences you write containing the keywords are substantially different from the original and focus on your own audience and purpose.

Use direct quotations sparingly, if at all. In most cases, they should not be longer than 75 words. All direct quotations must be set apart in the report text with quotation marks. Quoted passages longer than 75 words must also be set in a separate paragraph, single spaced, with margins increased to 2 inches (5 centimetres).

Cite your sources as you write. At the end of a paraphrased or quoted section, insert a citation in the format appropriate to your field. If you want to revise or move the paragraph or section later, simply move the citation with the text.

Most students know that they should cite direct quotations, but many miss the requirement to cite all paraphrased or graphic material. You provide a citation for all borrowed material, no matter what form it takes in your report.

2.4 REVISING

When you have finished the first draft, put your text away for a period. A break from looking at it will give you valuable perspective on what communicates and what does not. Be sure to leave enough time before your report deadline to have such a break.

Avoid printing several drafts of your unfinished report in order to revise and edit it. Practise reading and revising the text on your computer monitor. Your writing will go faster, and you will use less paper, an economical and environmentally sound practice.

Revising Your Text

When you come back to your draft, revise the content of it first. Check the sequence of main points to ensure they are complete and in the correct order. Get all the important detail into the report. Look again at secondary detail. With the full text written, you will have a better perspective on what to include. Remember to meet the needs of your audience and purpose. Check explanations of scientific and technical methods and principles. Are they too lengthy? Do they have enough detail? Revisions of content have the greatest impact on your reader. They will significantly improve the organization and readability of your report.

Next, revise the style of your report. Consider adding specific examples of general principles. Readers tend to focus on specific details and remember them. By remembering the specifics, they will understand the general principle behind them. For instance, Mickey Mouse is an example of the use of the principle of neoteny, the retention into adulthood of juvenile characteristics, to make Mickey less ratlike and more lovable.

Check to ensure that there are adequate transitions—words, sentences, and paragraphs that signal a change in topic or clarify relationships between ideas. Read over your descriptions for the shortest possible expression. We have a tendency to talk around ideas when we are unsure how to express them, which creates more words than necessary in a first draft. Written work should be concise: the right number of words to express the idea, no more and no less. Cut wordy language in favour of short, direct language; for example, replace "due to the fact that" with "because."

Using Good Scientific and Technical Writing Style

Know your writing goals and keep them in mind as you review your drafts. The following qualities are characteristic of all good scientific and technical writing. Your revisions should develop these qualities.

- *Accuracy.* Record facts carefully in lab work and in the field. Do the same when researching the literature: read and record your sources accurately. Be objective and free of bias. Scientific and technical writing must be reasonable, fair, and honest.
- *Accessibility.* Make it easy for your reader to locate information in your writing. Write in small, independent sections. Use an outline of headings showing main topics divided logically into smaller units. Use the elements of the front and back matter to show where to find these topics in your report.
- *Comprehensiveness.* Provide all information that the reader will need: background, methods, principal findings, conclusions, and recommendations. Good scientific and technical reporting is comprehensive; report all information that you consider relevant to your topic. Remember that your reader will use the information in your report. The detail you describe must meet the reader's needs effectively, efficiently, and safely in the case of lab or field procedures with a safety element, such as the handling of harmful chemicals. Since a report is also a record of projects, meetings, or events, it should be as comprehensive as possible so that a company or agency has all the information it needs to evaluate and plan projects.
- *Clarity.* Your final product should convey a single meaning that readers can understand easily. Words can have multiple meanings. Ambiguity can be good in creative writing, but it is bad in scientific and technical writing. Unclear technical writing is expensive, breaks down cooperation, and can be dangerous.
- *Correctness.* A convention is the way people usually do things. Language has conventions: grammar, spelling, punctuation, and usage.

Documents have format conventions, such as letters, memos, and reports. Learn the conventions and apply them. Readers of scientific and technical literature around the world use many different kinds of English. To communicate with them, it is essential to write in standard, conventional English.

Avoiding the Passive Voice

Some scientific writers will tell you to use the passive voice in every sentence of your report; for example, "It was observed that the male lionfish was inactive when it was fed during daylight hours."

While this style was acceptable in the past, mainly to project the objectivity of the scientist, it is not the current style. Using the passive voice throughout your text leads to loss of clarity, awkward phrasing, and needless length and complexity of sentences.

The modern style is to combine the third-person, active voice appropriately with the passive voice in order to focus the reader on the scientific and technical principles and processes discussed in the report. Consider the following example: "The logs float into the catch basin and are hauled into the mill by a chain conveyor." This sentence focuses attention on the logs at the centre of the milling process by using both active and passive voices.

Creating a Formal Tone

Reports are formal in tone. Check the drafts of your report for the following characteristics to create a formal tone.

- Use the third person primarily; for example, "The investigations included a control plot of mixed conifers planted at intermediate spacings." Avoid the first and second persons; for example, "We included in our investigation a control plot of mixed conifers planted at intermediate spacings" or "You must include in your investigation a control plot of mixed conifers planted at intermediate spacings."
- Use the past tense except when describing universal processes, such as the following: "Changes in water temperature reduce resistance in the sensor and increase current flow in the meter circuit."
- Avoid contractions—"don't," "they'll," "I've," and so on.

2.5 EDITING

Editing is correcting. Writing in correct, standard English communicates to a wide audience, including those for whom English is not a first language. Mistakes in style, grammar, and usage can come from a variety of sources. Be aware of the mistakes you typically make and check your report draft carefully to identify and eliminate them.

Using Correct Language

Correct language is clear language. Violations of standard English will muddy your meaning and suggest ignorance. If you write "I seen" and "I done," or confuse the verbs "lie" and "lay," or say "myself" when you mean "I" or "me," your audience will assume you know no better. Worse, your audience will begin to focus attention on your mistakes and miss what you have to say.

Correct language is learned in steps. First, learn the types of words found in an English sentence: verbs, nouns, adjectives, adverbs, prepositions, conjunctions, and so on. Second, learn the uses of words and groups of words in an English sentence: subject, predicate, object, phrase, clause, participle, gerund, and so on. Third, learn some fault analysis. Most errors are common, such as comma splices and sentence fragments. Learn the ones that you tend to make and look for them in your report drafts.

Correct language is a responsibility of all report writers. Do not make the mistake of thinking of correctness as a "basic" skill. Writing clear, clean descriptions in a report does not come naturally. It is the product of hard work and attention to detail, qualities that also make a good scientist or technician.

Correct language is consistent. When you make choices of style, vocabulary, technical terms, spelling, and so on, make them consciously and consistently the same from one paragraph of the report through to another. Inconsistencies create confusion and misunderstanding. Read your text over, looking for consistency in your language.

Help with language problems is available on many Internet sites. Campus libraries have good textbooks on technical writing with grammar help, as well as handbooks of Canadian English indexed to specific problems of grammar and writing style. Campus and commercial bookstores carry dictionaries of Canadian English and quick grammar guides. Use them.

Appendix A, found toward the end of this book, is a general guide to correct English. In the following section, we look at some forms of language that are specific to scientific and technical writing.

Technical Conventions

The Use of Numbers

The scientific and technical writer must include many quantities in the text of a report. Learn the conventions of technical style to help you decide whether to write the quantity as a numeral or in words.

1 • Use numerals for quantities combined with units of measurement: 500 rpm.
2 • Use Arabic numerals for quantities of 10 or greater. If no other rule applies, write quantities less than 10 in words.
3 • Use numerals for all quantities in a series, that is, a list of quantified items in a sentence, such as "They used 8 thinning saws, 241 of paint, and 215 units of stock."
4 • Use numerals for times of the day, days of the month, quantities of money, decimal expressions, and percentages.
5 • Do not begin a sentence with a numeral. Either write out the quantity in words or rewrite the sentence.

Write approximations or indefinite measurements in words. The language must clearly indicate that an approximation is intended; for example, "The final distribution figures included *approximately* forty more samples from the refinery." Use approximations sparingly. Write very large quantities in a form combining numerals and words, such as $23.4 million.

In compound number adjectives, write out the first number or the shorter number and use a numeral for the other: "twenty 16-cm trout."

The Use of Abbreviations

Abbreviate units of measurement, names for technical materials, and names of organizations when it is appropriate. Learn commonly accepted abbreviations for units of measurement in your field of study. Follow these rules:

6 • Abbreviate units of measurement following numerals denoting an exact quantity (18 ha, 2700 l).
7 • Write abbreviations in the singular only (2700 rpm).
8 • Use lowercase letters for abbreviations except for letters standing for proper nouns or adjectives or those capitalized by convention (180 psi, 2400 Btu, 147.060 MHz).

♌ • Do not use periods after abbreviations, except when the abbreviation spells a word. Do not use signs, that is, visual symbols, for abbreviations. Exceptions include conventional use, such as the percent symbol in "28%" or the degree symbol in "45° north latitude," as well as symbols in tables and figures.

♋ • Abbreviate names of organizations and nontechnical terms as long as the first mention gives the full title. Form these abbreviations without periods or spacing; for example, American Radio Relay League (ARRL), or fibreglass-reinforced plastic (FRP). Such abbreviations are called acronyms.

The Use of Hyphens

Hyphens are used to form compound words. The technical writer uses many compound expressions for technical concepts and measurements. Therefore, he or she must know when to hyphenate such compounds. However, a distinct difference between American and British usage of hyphens often creates confusion for the Canadian writer. The Canadian writer should generally follow British usage.

In general, write prefixes solid with the root word, as in pre + determined = predetermined. Note the following exceptions:

- to permit internal capitalization, as in pre-Cambrian
- to aid pronunciation, as in re-allocate, re-form (meaning "to form again")
- "self," as in self-closing doors.

Hyphenate compound adjectives, but do not hyphenate compound nouns; for example, a sodium-chloride solution, but sodium chloride; a flow-chart evaluation, but a flow chart. Hyphenate to avoid ambiguity, that is; for example, two-hundred gallon drums versus two hundred-gallon drums.

Never hyphenate a compound formed with an adverb; for example, a badly managed operation. When uncertain, observe dictionary usage.

Scientific Usage

The International System of Units (SI)

The International System of Units is the accepted form of the metric system that is advocated by the Canadian Standards Association (CSA) and is the official system of measurements for Canada. A complete list of units is available from Natural Resources Canada in the "GSC Guide to Authors: The International System of Units."

The Use of Species Names

Give the scientific name, together with the authority for that name, following the first mention of any common name for a species. This eliminates confusion arising from the use of a variety of common names for the same species. After the first mention, the common name may be used alone. Species names in the abstract, one of the elements of front matter in a scientific report, must also include both common and scientific names.

Use capital letters in common names only for proper nouns, that is, those that name a person, place, or thing. Here are some examples:

- black spruce (*Picea mariana [Mill-] B.S.P.*)
- Norway spruce (*Picea abies [L.] Karst.*)
- bunchberry (*Comus canadensis L.*)
- spruce budworm (*Choristoneura fumiferana [Clem.]*).

Italicize the Latin words used in scientific names. Capitalize the generic name but not the specific. Consult taxonomies of species for the correct abbreviations for the names of authorities.

Mathematical Equations

Space all mathematical equations on separate lines away from the text. Centre short equations. Begin longer ones flush with the left-hand margin and continue them, if necessary, on the second and successive lines indented two spaces.

Number long equations and formulas in the text. Place a numeral in round brackets on the line below the equation and on the right margin of the page. When referring to the equation in the text, use the form "Equation (5)," where 5 is the equation number assigned in sequence through the report.

Insert mathematical equations into your text using the Microsoft Equation Editor. See Appendix D for a tutorial on the use of the Equation Editor.

The formula for heat flow under these conditions is

$$Q = \frac{k(T_1 - T_2)At}{d}$$

(5)

where

Q =   heat flow,

k =   coefficient of thermal conductivity for the refractory material,

$T_1 - T_2$ =   temperature drop from hot face to cold face,

A =   area of the wall,

t =   time,

d =   thickness of the wall.

Box 2.1: Format for Mathematical Equations

CHECKLIST FOR THE REPORT-WRITING PROCESS

Steps in Report Writing

- Gather all available research materials.
- Plan before you write.
- Draft the main points of the body.
- Write your concluding sections.
- Add your graphic elements.
- Write your introduction.
- Write the report elements.

During the report-writing process, be sure that you have done the following:

- Completed all necessary research.
- Made research notes with clearly written paraphrases and bibliographic information about all secondary sources.
- Organized information into coherent, logical outline of headings.
- Learned and used the capabilities of word processing software.
- Drafted text using information from notes and following the outline.
- Checked your use of secondary sources, reading all paraphrased sections for originality, making sure that no passages are too close, double-checking that sources are cited and listed.
- In your use of primary sources, checked that you used exact quantities and measurements and that you have included accurate data.
- Written short, coherent paragraphs and divided text into sections written with logical, descriptive headings.
- Revised your draft, checking content, amount of detail, specific examples, and transitions.
- Used good technical writing style, with writing that is accurate, accessible, comprehensive, clear, and correct.
- Restricted your use of passive voice.

- Used an appropriate tone, with formal language, third-person sentences, and past tense.
- Identified and eliminated grammatical errors, such as fragments, run-on sentences, disagreements of subject–predicate and pronoun–antecedent, errors in the principal parts of verbs, and misplaced or dangling modifiers.
- Corrected punctuation errors.
- Corrected stylistic errors, checking pronoun references, diction, and parallelism.
- Checked usage and eliminated errors, paying specific attention to easily confused words, such as accept/except, amount/number, effect/affect, if/whether, principle/principal.
- Spell-checked your document and then proofread it, looking up misspelled words and making sure that you used Canadian spellings.
- Used technical conventions and double-checked your use of numbers, abbreviations, and hyphens, as well as metric (SI) units, scientific names of species, and mathematical equations.

Chapter

Formatting Your Report

3

Overview: This chapter describes how to format informal and formal reports and how to set up illustrations to support your written descriptions of scientific and technical work. The discussion covers the typical sequence of information as well as the physical form of a report, including page format and report elements. A description of letter, memo, and e-mail formats is included.

3.1 REPORT STRUCTURE

According to semanticist Dr. S.I. Hayakawa (Hayakawa and Hayakawa, 1989), we can make only three kinds of statements with language: a report, an inference, and a judgment. A report is a statement of fact; it is verifiable. An inference is a conclusion we draw about what we do not know based on what we do know. A judgment is a statement of opinion, about what we like or dislike. People often confuse these three, thinking that a sentence such as "This type of instrument is no good" is a statement of fact when it is really an opinion. Structure your scientific or technical reports to separate and focus on each of these three kinds of statements in distinct, clearly labelled sections.

The body of a report contains descriptions of scientific and technical methods used to investigate problems or to gather data. It also describes the results of investigations, usually with tables of data. This is the reporting function essential to technical writing. Information must be accurate, complete, and presented in simple, clear language with appropriate tables and figures.

The body also usually contains some analysis of the problem or data. This analysis consists of inferences—that is, conclusions that you draw based on evidence. Secondary sources and standard mathematical formulas, such as chi-square analysis, will help you reach accurate, logical conclusions. Note that reasoning through to a valid conclusion is never easy. Give yourself time to think and to rewrite the concluding section several times. Your education and work experience will be invaluable in this process.

The body of the report may also contain a section of recommendations at the end. Do not include a section of recommendations unless your intended reader, usually your boss, has specifically asked you to do so. Recommendations are your opinions. We all make judgments about our experiences. However, the reader of scientific and technical writing will consider only judgments based on carefully reported facts and logical conclusions. If you conduct your investigations carefully, write up the detail plainly, analyze the data correctly, and recommend an option that fits the data and analysis, your supervisor will be more likely to follow your recommendation.

3.2 INFORMAL REPORTS: LETTER AND MEMO REPORTS

The most common reports in the workplace are the short ones. Regular communication of scientific and technical information is essential to effective operation of a business or government agency. Employees responsible for such information typically communicate it in the form of letters or memos, now sent routinely as e-mail. The following section outlines form and content of letters and memos. Write letters to people outside your company or agency; write memos to people inside your company or agency. Use e-mail for both sets of correspondents.

Writing Letters

Letters are brief communications on a single topic sent in a conventional format to a reader outside your company or organization. Letter language and format developed in the 18th century and continues to evolve. Contemporary practice has retained some traditional elements and introduced new ones as technology and business needs have changed. Learn these basic elements and then learn how to be flexible with them, depending on your message and your reader. At all times, write a strong letter by following sound principles of English composition.

Letter Format

Letters have conventional parts. Familiarize yourself with them and learn how to set them up in your word processing software. The following example shows the correct form of a letter in full block format, which is the most commonly used and easiest to write.

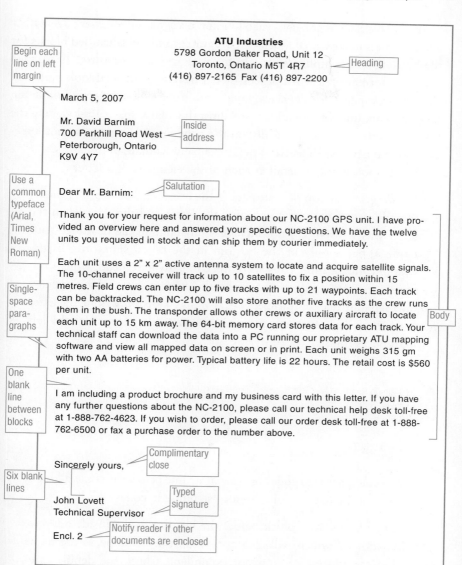

Box 3.1: Block-Format Letter

The full block format begins each line at the left margin of your page. Other letter formats make use of indented paragraphs and right-justified blocks for the heading and complimentary closing with a typed signature. These take longer to format on a word processor but have a traditional look preferred by some companies or agencies. Single-space the blocks of type in a letter, leaving blank lines between blocks. Adjust this blank space after writing the letter to centre the text vertically on the page. Use a single, common typeface for the letter, such as Arial or Times New Roman.

Let us look in more detail at each of the elements of a letter.

- *Heading.* At the top of your page is the heading. The heading shows the address of the person sending the letter and the date when the letter was written. Do not include your name in the heading. Your name appears only at the bottom in the typed signature. In the example, the heading consists of the company letterhead, which contains the contact information, and the current date, which appears on a separate line several spaces below. If you are not writing the letter from your desk at work, use your return address typed at the left margin, as follows:

316 Ritson Road
Oshawa, Ontario
L1G 5P8

March 5, 2007

Put Canadian postal codes on a separate line below the street address. Write out the date in full; do not use numeric codes.

- *Inside address.* The block below the heading is the inside address. This address, which will also appear on the envelope, is the name and street address of your correspondent. Check the details carefully, especially the name and title. Whenever possible, address your letter to a specific person—someone who has the expertise and the authority to act on your letter. If no specific person is available, address it to a position, such as: "The Personnel Manager," "Network Manager," "Director of Information Services," and so on. The least desirable option is to address the letter to a large company; such letters, if answered at all, are often answered by someone not in a position to help you. If you must address a company, add an attention line below the inside address to direct the letter to a specific person.

- *Salutation.* The "Dear Somebody" part of the letter is the salutation. Salutations are conventional and must agree with the first line of the inside address. When addressing a specific person, use his or her name as you find it; for example, "Dear Adrianna Taylor." When addressing a position, use "Dear Sir or Madam." When addressing a company, use "Ladies and Gentlemen." Follow the salutation with a colon.
- *Body.* Type the body of the letter in single-spaced paragraphs beginning at the left margin. Leave a blank line between paragraphs. Letter paragraphs must be short.
- *Complimentary close.* After the letter body, type a complimentary close. Begin with a capital letter and end with a comma. Use conventional lines that most readers recognize, such as "Sincerely yours," "Yours truly," and so on. Leave about six blank lines for your signature, then type your name as you wish others to use it. Include your position with your company or agency if this will help your reader identify you and your concerns. If you intend to include other material with the letter in the mailing envelope, leave a blank line below your typed signature and type the word "Enclosure" to signal to the reader that something else is in the envelope. You may abbreviate this to "Encl." and add a numeral to indicate the number of enclosures.

Composing Letters

Letters should always address a single issue. Do not attempt to compose a letter that deals with more than one major subject. Follow the writing process when composing a letter: consider your audience and purpose, gather all necessary information, sketch an outline of paragraphs, and compose the letter of short paragraphs with strong, clear topic sentences. Deciding on your purpose for writing the letter and expressing it clearly in the opening paragraph is the most important factor in writing a successful letter.

Write an opening paragraph that states clearly the purpose of the letter. Use action words, as in the following examples: "to review the budget for the field instrumentation project," "to summarize the lab testing data gathered to date," "to provide the input you requested for staffing needs in July and August." Do not introduce yourself; your name and position will appear in the letter as the typed signature. Keep the opening paragraph short.

Include the details of the letter in the middle paragraphs. Scientific and technical information about principles and processes can be complex. Therefore, group your details into focused, logically connected topics and write a short paragraph about each one.

Write a concluding paragraph that indicates clearly the response you want from your reader. Business letters ask the reader to do something or think something. Know your audience and your reasons for writing the letter. Express your expectations clearly and courteously in the closing paragraph. Again, use action words, as in these examples: "Please send the requested information to the address above," "If you have concerns about the new data, please contact me by return mail," or "Please let me know your decision with regard to staffing as soon as the summer budget has been approved."

Letters can be quite brief. A follow-up letter from ATU Industries might look as follows. (See Box 3.2)

Notice that the three sentences economically accomplish the objectives of a business letter: purpose stated, business details, and action required.

When you have finished composing, formatting, and revising the letter, print a copy and sign it in the space between the complimentary close and the typed signature.

Writing Memos

Organizations use memos for internal communication. Memos provide permanent file records of activity and decisions made. They communicate routine news to individuals throughout an organization, summarizing key information and suggesting action. Use memos for brief scientific or technical reports that include sections written under headings and graphic presentations of data.

Memo Format

The conventional memo begins with four lines of text, each introduced with standard guidewords, such as the following:

To:
From:
Subject:
Date:

ATU Industries
5798 Gordon Baker Road, Unit 12
Don Mills, Ontario M5T 4R7
(416) 897-2165 Fax (416) 897-2200

March 15, 2007

Mr. David Barnim
700 Parkhill Road West
Peterborough, Ontario
K9V 4Y7

Dear Mr. Barnim:

Thank you for your order on March 14.

It will take four to six business days to pack and ship your GPS units by courier.

Payment is due in 30 days.

Sincerely yours,

John Lovett
Technical Supervisor

Box 3.2: Follow-Up Letter

Write the body of a memo in block form, starting each line at the left margin. Use single spacing, with a blank line between paragraphs, as in the following example.

MEMORANDUM

TO: Gary Farrow, Manager, Lab Services
FROM: Leah McVeigh, Titration Lab Technician
SUBJECT: Revised Procedure for Equilibrium Titration
DATE: February 15, 2007

In line with our upgrade of water testing facilities, we have purchased a new resonance biosensor for equilibrium titration of water samples. The following is the revised procedure that we are using with the new biosensor. Preliminary results suggest that we are getting measurements that are more accurate for a wider range of potential pathogens.

The new procedure is as follows:

1. Arrange a closed loop with two micro flex loops and two stoppered flasks.
2. Connect the external syringe pump to one of the stoppered flasks.
3. Set up the biosensor unit and insert the two sensor spots at opposite ends of the closed loop. One sensor binds interactive molecules in the fluid passing over it, while the other serves as a reference value for total units.
4. Inject a 15 cc water sample.
5. Activate the syringe pump and check for continuous circulation of the sample.
6. Activate the biosensor and record differential readings from the display.
7. Draw off a 2 cc sample and perform a standard stepwise titration.
8. Multiply the titration results by the biosensor readings.

The new sensor gives readings that are more consistent over a wider range of temperatures and water conditions and requires simpler operating steps. If you wish, we will arrange a demonstration in the lab at your convenience. A report comparing titration results with the old and new methods is being prepared. Please call if you have any questions.

Box 3.3: Memo

You may choose to sign a memo to lend weight to an important directive. You may introduce a memo with the word "Memorandum" to identify the type of communication, with the company logo, or with personalized information. You may also wish to insert a graphic line below the guide-words to separate the heading visually from the body of the memo.

Composing Memos

As with letters, write memos on one subject only. Do not deal with several issues in a single memo.

Begin the memo with a short, direct statement of your purpose in writing. Use action words, such as "to request," "to explain," "to authorize," and so on. Add any necessary explanations; for example, "This request for a change in scheduling is the result of a shortage of parts at the main supplier's warehouse."

The middle part of a technical memo can be several paragraphs long, describing specific details of processes and products. For this reason, technical memos can have two or three pages. Insert a descriptive heading at the beginning of each major topic covered in multipage memos. Check your paragraphs to make sure they are short, describe only one topic each, and follow in a logical sequence.

Technical memos can also include illustrations, such as brief figures that explain processes or show how devices function or brief tables that summarize data or compare technical parameters. Use bulleted or numbered lists wherever possible.

In the last paragraph of your memo, describe the action you want your reader to take, such as returning a questionnaire or discussing the memo's information with staff. Provide contact information. Make sure your reader knows how you wish to be contacted and is aware of any deadlines associated with the requested action.

Common Types of Memos

Organizations use specific types of memos to communicate in common workplace situations.

A directive memo defines a policy or procedure for your readers to follow. Typically, you will send this memo as a supervisor to your staff. When composing the directive memo, explain first the reasons for the directive and then state it as a request; for example, "Please submit all timesheets and invoices for this phase of the research before May 1." A polite tone works best.

A response to an inquiry provides information requested by someone in your organization. Open with your purpose: to respond to a request for information. Summarize the content briefly. Then discuss the detail that is requested. Scientific and technical information can be difficult to explain, especially in a memo, so be sure to organize the content of your explanations and descriptions into short, logically sequenced paragraphs. Close with a request for a response, if needed, or an offer to assist with information at a future date.

A trip report is a record of a business trip. Organizations require these to account for travel funds, to record observations made in the field, or to report on meetings held with clients and associates in other places. Report only important details.

Field and lab reports provide supervisory staff with the results of inspection and maintenance procedures. The memo should include the purpose of the work, the problem or hypothesis that you investigated and the methods you used to do so, a description of the steps in the investigation, a summary of the results, and recommendations, if required.

A request memo asks someone in your organization for information. Start the memo with a direct request and explain the reasons for it. Most requests for scientific or technical information require detailed and specific answers. Therefore, it is best to present the particular areas of concern as a bulleted list of specific, detailed questions. Vague questions get vague, unhelpful answers. Close with a reasonable deadline by which you need the information and the method by which you wish to receive the reply.

Writing E-Mails

E-mails are electronic forms of letters and memos, distributed from your workstation over the company's local network or the Internet.

The Importance of E-Mails

E-mails are formal documents. Students become accustomed to informality in personal e-mail, including the use of short forms, capital letters, emoticons, and bad spelling and grammar. You must curb these habits in the workplace.

Communications dealing with scientific and technical subjects must be accurate. The rules of good writing apply to electronic communication. Any message you send reveals your personality and the quality of your work.

E-mails are not private. They are stored as files accessible by others. Network software can allow supervisors to see what you have sent and received. Inappropriate form or content, then, can hurt your career. Treat e-mail as you would treat a formal memo.

Composing E-Mails

E-mail software provides the standard guidewords used in memos. Most important of these is the subject line. Do not write vague or confusing subject lines. Most readers must prioritize hundreds of daily e-mails, separating spam and routine communication from more urgent workplace concerns. Your subject line is the only clue your reader has about the content and urgency of your e-mail. To write a good subject line, write the e-mail first, then use the keywords from your message to build a short description that communicates the main point.

Send e-mail messages only to those people who need to receive them. E-mail address books and listservs make it easy to send a message to dozens of people, many of whom do not need the information. Be careful when replying to a listserv message. Clicking the reply button will send your e-mail to everyone on the list, even though you intend your reply only for the originator of the message.

Keep messages short. As a rule of thumb, fill one screen, or about 25 lines, for routine messages. Scientific and technical information will require more text.

For detailed e-mails on scientific and technical subjects, work out the paragraphs on a word processor and paste them into your e-mail software. For longer documents and graphics, attach text and graphic files to a short, explanatory e-mail that identifies the purpose, content, and file format of each of the attachments.

Proofread every e-mail you send. Most people find proofreading on a computer screen more difficult than on paper. The technology pushes us to get things done faster without taking the necessary time to think through the issues, from content to logical sequence to correct language. Writing in a rush can lead to miscommunication when the words do not express accurately what we intend to say. Miscommunication causes wasted effort and resources. The more important the message, the more time you need to write it. Always think twice about your message before you click the "Send" icon.

Writing Short Reports

As noted in Chapter 1, the word *report* comes from Latin words that mean "to carry back." The purpose of a report is to carry back important information in a written form. The information that you carry back to supervisors from lab or field investigations is essential to their administrative work. Choose the memo, short report, or long report form based on the amount and complexity of your message, remembering always to be as concise as possible.

Many lab and field reports begin as fill-in-the-blank forms. Gather information using appropriate lab or field procedures so that you can analyze results accurately. Recently, written forms have been adapted for handheld data recorders, which allows users to electronically manipulate the resulting files.

Short Report Format

Short reports are usually between 5 and 15 pages long in manuscript form. For reports less than 5 pages, write a 2-page, single-spaced letter or memo. For reports more than 15 pages, consider adding more report elements to keep track of increasingly complex content.

A short report requires few formal elements. Typical short reports that contain only primary research include the following:

- title page
- abstract
- introduction
- body, divided into sections with descriptive headings
- conclusion
- appendix.

You will find complete descriptions of these elements in the section on elements of the formal report later on in this chapter.

3.3 FORMAL REPORTS

Formal reports are longer than routine documents, usually 20 pages or more. They deal with complex scientific and technical issues; therefore, they require additional formal elements, such as an index or a glossary, which provide access to the information and promote understanding of the report's content. In addition, they require a letter or memorandum of transmittal to shift responsibility for the contents of the report to a specific reader or readers.

Formatting Formal Reports

Format for reports is similar to the traditional form of manuscripts: double-spaced text on good-quality paper, 8½ by 11 inches. Before looking at details of page format, let us briefly consider the use of word processing technology in this context.

Word Processing

Format report pages using available technologies, including word processing software and laser or inkjet printing. Acquiring good keyboarding skills will make your work more efficient, so it is worthwhile to invest time in learning to type if you have not already done so. As well, learn your word processing software thoroughly; it will make your job of formatting the report much easier.

Writing a report on a computer requires you to use both keyboarding and composition skills. Keyboarding can be quick and efficient; thinking through your writing issues is often not as quick. Do not let the computer's speed push you into preparing a document without the necessary revising, editing, and proofreading steps. Allow sufficient time to complete your research, to compose clear text at the keyboard, and to revise the text to make it readable. It also helps to ask a knowledgeable person to review the manuscript for you.

Spacing and Margins

Use double spacing in your report. Reserve single spacing for specific elements, such as the abstract, long quotations, vertical lists, and entries in the reference list. Note that business reports often have 1.5 line spacing instead of double spacing.

Indent the first line of each paragraph about five spaces. Do not write block paragraphs without indentation.

Do not allow the first line of a paragraph to sit alone at the bottom of a page (orphan line) or the last line of a paragraph to sit alone at the top of a page (widow line). Do not allow main headings or subheadings to sit alone at the bottom of a page.

Use the default margins in your word processing software. Direct quotations of secondary sources longer than 75 words are usually set single-spaced within wider margins. However, such long text passages are not desirable in scientific writing.

Typefaces

Use a standard serif or sans serif typeface such as Times New Roman or Arial. These are Microsoft TrueType™ fonts that most word processing software can read and print easily. They are also easy for your readers to see.

Typefaces should be 10, 11, or 12 points. Anything smaller is difficult to read. Anything larger uses more pages than necessary. Note that actual typeface size varies with design and leading. Text in a 12-point Garamond typeface takes less room than the same text using 12-point Century Schoolbook typeface.

Headings

Write the text of your report under descriptive headings. Organize your content into an outline of descriptive headings with at least two levels of organization. If you can group any section of your report into a third level of headings, do so. Such a grouping will help you understand the content better, and it will help your reader do the same. Look at the headings in the sample student report in Appendix E.

How many main headings should you have? Divide your content into three or four main topic areas, and use the keywords from these topic areas to create descriptive headings. A report of moderate length will have about six main headings and a series of subheadings.

In the workplace, reports can be longer than the typical 2 000-word college paper. Such reports will require more organization and more main headings.

In the body of the report, place the first heading, which should be "Introduction," at the top of the first page. Place the other headings above the paragraphs of relevant text, in the logical order you have chosen. Do not place each new main heading on a new page, as this wastes paper and adds nothing to the layout of the document.

Headings are the first and most important access point for your reader into the content of your report. Therefore, you must set the headings apart from the text using simple graphic levels of hierarchy. Use the following system:

MAIN HEADING

Subheading
    Third-level Heading

Boldfaced headings stand out clearly from the body typeface. To differentiate headings further from body text, you can use an alternate typeface that is close in design to the base font of the report. An example would be the use of the sans serif Tahoma font for headings with the sans serif Arial base font.

If you plan to refer frequently to other report sections within your report text, you may number report headings with the decimal system of numbering, illustrated below.

1.0 MAIN HEADING

1.1 Subheading
    1.1.1 Third-level Heading

Note that heading styles, including design and numbering, vary considerably according to company or agency practice. Consult written guidelines or style manuals designed for documents submitted in your specific situation.

Page Numbering

Number the pages of the front matter if you have included three elements or more. Do not place a number on the title page, although it is the first page. On subsequent pages, use lowercase Roman numerals centred at the bottom of the page. Appendix D describes how to number pages in Microsoft Word XP.

Put page numbers of the report body in the upper-right corner. Use Arabic numerals. Begin page numbering with the first page of text, the report introduction. It is not necessary to alternate page numbers between the upper-right and -left corners, since the reports will be printed on one side of the page only.

Report Presentation

College professors usually accept reports and essays stapled in the upper-left corner. Be sure you have assembled the elements of the report in the correct order before stapling and do not fold your report.

Some college courses and most workplace situations require report presentations that are more formal, such as envelopes or report covers. Add a label to each envelope or report cover showing the report title, the author, the person or group to whom you are submitting the report, and the deadline date.

Report covers may be heavy paper, vinyl, or clear plastic. Some college courses and workplace readers will accept clear plastic covers with a plastic wedge spine or report covers that require you to three-hole punch your report pages. The most widely acceptable format for report covers, though also more expensive, is spiral binding. With this type of presentation, the report pages will lie flat.

Elements of Formal Reports

This section examines the various elements that make up a formal report. For examples of how these report elements should look when formatted, consult the student paper in Appendix E. One general guideline is that you should put each element of the front and back matter on a separate page but write the elements of the body on continuous pages.

Title Page

Centre the lines of the title page between the right and left margins. Space the title page elements vertically equidistant from each other. Leave at least four blank lines from the top margin to the title and four blank lines from the bottom margin to the date at the bottom.

Write the four required elements on the title page in the following order:

1. *Title* should be long enough to be fully descriptive of the content and should include all keywords.

2. *Author name* goes under a "By" line underneath the title. Write the name or names of the person or persons responsible for the paper. You may want to include their formal titles and departments.

3. *Destination* goes under a "To" line. Write the name of the person or persons responsible for reading the report and who take responsibility for acting on its contents.

4. *Date* should be written out in full, without numeric coding. Write the deadline date or the current date if you are submitting the report before the deadline.

The title page may contain other information, such as a company logo or report serial number. Add such elements as you require them. Do not place graphic images on the title page.

**THE DEVELOPMENT OF MAYAN EPIGRAPHY
AND ITS IMPACT ON INTERPRETATION OF CLASSIC
MAYA CULTURE**

By

Jonathan L. White

To

Professor C. L. Gulston

October 23, 2004

Box 3.4: Title Page

Table of Contents

Centre the heading "TABLE OF CONTENTS" in bold capital letters.

In a column on the left, add the elements of the front matter that come after the contents page, the descriptive headings in the body, and the reference list. Include the appendix in the list if you have included one in your report. Single-space your entries.

In a column on the right, opposite each heading, list the page number where the reader can find that heading. List only the starting page number for each section; an ending page number is not needed.

Insert leader dots to connect the headings with their page numbers. Appendix D describes how to use leader dots in Microsoft Word XP. Add the heading "Page" over the page number column.

List of Illustrations

Centre the heading "LIST OF ILLUSTRATIONS" in bold capital letters. You may also call this element "Illustrations" or "List of Tables and Figures," using the latter for longer lists subdivided into a list of tables and a list of figures.

In a column on the left, add the figure or table number and title for each of the illustrations in the body of your report. Do not include illustrations placed in the appendix. Double-space your entries.

In a column on the right, opposite each entry, list the page number where your reader can find that figure or table. Insert leader dots connecting the headings with their page numbers. Add the heading "Page" over the page number column.

Abstract

A descriptive abstract is a brief summary of the report's content, about 250 words long. It is a separate element of the report. Place the abstract in the report immediately following the List of Illustrations.

Centre the title "ABSTRACT" at the top of the page. Single-space the abstract text below the heading.

The abstract summarizes the following content of the report:

- research goal or goals and the questions answered by your investigation
- research methods, including both field work and searches of literature
- results, including the main topic covered in your report and any analysis of field or lab work (do not refer to your data or discuss the details here)
- main conclusions, including reflection on the material presented in the report.

TABLE OF CONTENTS

Page

ii

Box 3.5: Table of Contents

LIST OF ILLUSTRATIONS

Page

iii

Box 3.6: List of Illustrations

The abstract must be an independent summary that does not require the reader to look up references to the text of the report. The abstract is not an introduction. Its tone is objective, and it is written in the past tense—a look back at the completed project, not a look forward at the report to come.

An informative abstract may be longer, up to 400 words, including a summary of the report's recommendations.

Report Body

Divide your report into separate sections. Use bold headings and subheadings to identify the content of each section. Write topic headings. Do not use sentences or questions for headings.

Reports have a beginning, a middle, and an end—that is, an introduction, a part that contains the main content, and a conclusion. Below are details about these main three sections of the body of a report.

Introduction

Begin your report body with the heading "Introduction." Start numbering pages here with Arabic numerals in the upper-right corner. Do not put the report title on the first page of the body.

The purpose of the introduction is to answer a reader's questions about the report's content: "What is the report about?" "How was the information gathered?" "What was the purpose?" "How much information is here?" You can answer each of these typical reader questions in a separate subsection of your introduction.

Insert the following descriptive subheadings into your introduction to identify the topics of concern to your reader.

- *Purpose and Scope.* Describe the primary goals of your research. Add a description of any secondary goals, such as providing information to a supervisor, reporting to a safety committee, or completing requirements for a college course. Describe the scope of your investigation. Time and resources limit field or lab work. Explain those limits and the specific questions that your work addresses. Time and resources also limit library research. Describe the specific topics for which you have research information. Include a plan of development of the main topics covered by the report.

ABSTRACT

The purpose of this investigation is to summarize current knowledge of Maya writing, the forms that Maya writing takes, and the history of the decipherment of Maya writing. To illustrate these points, this paper describes Maya glyphs found at three major sites of the Classic Maya. Sources for this paper include books by Michael Coe and Norman Hammond on Maya history, writing, and epigraphy, as well as a number of Internet web sites.

Four Maya codices currently exist, the largest being the Madrid Codex. The majority of glyphs are found on limestone stelae at the major city sites of the Classic Maya. In addition, glyphs are found in wall murals and specialized structures like the hieroglyphic stair at Copan. Glyphs include symbols for numerals, people, and language phonemes.

Tatiana Proskouriakoff discovered the key to deciphering Maya glyphs in the 1950s. Recent work by the late Linda Schele and David Stuart has increased our understanding of Maya writing to include about 85% of extant glyphs. The glyphs on monuments at Copan, Tikal, and Palenque all tell the history of the rulers of those cities, their families, and their personal achievements. The deciphering of Maya texts has significantly altered our interpretation of classic Maya civilization.

iv

Box 3.7: Abstract

1

INTRODUCTION

Purpose and Scope

The purpose of this investigation is to summarize current knowledge of Maya hieroglyphic writing, the forms that Maya writing takes, and the history of the decipherment of Maya writing. To illustrate these points, this paper describes Maya glyphs found at three major sites of the Classic Maya.

The scope of the investigation is limited to the significant details of Maya written texts and the history of efforts to decipher them. This includes significant changes in our view of Maya history and culture that have come about because of deciphering Maya writing.

Box 3.8: Introduction

- *Methodology.* Describe the field or lab techniques that you applied in order to get the data you are presenting. Most of these will be standard techniques recognizable by scientific and technical readers in your field, so you need to only name the technique. If you have modified the technique to suit the goals, study area, or instrumentation available, indicate these modifications here.
- *Review of Literature.* Describe and evaluate the secondary sources you used. Name your sources and describe how they contributed to the final report. Organize your description in more-to-less-important order, starting with the sources that were most authoritative, up-to-date, and complete. It is not necessary to discuss all the sources that you read, such as general background information that did not get included in the report. When referring to book and report titles, capitalize the important words and place the title in italic typeface; for example, "The proceedings are called *Growth and Utilization of Poplars in Canada*, published in 1999." When referring to journal or magazine articles, enclose the title in quotation marks.
- *Study Area.* If you are reporting on field work or a subject with a geographical dimension, include this section in your report and supply a map and a written description orienting the reader to the study area.
- *Background.* Include this section to describe state-of-the-art techniques or equipment that you used in the reported work. Use this section to list personnel, equipment, weather conditions, and working conditions where these may have affected the analysis of your data.

Review of Literature
Keep the sections of your introduction brief. You can develop important points in detail in the main body of the report. The purpose of the introduction is to give your reader an overview, a mental roadmap to follow as he or she reads, as well as a rationale for the work and any background information required for understanding the reported results.

Report Content
The sections after the introduction describe the new information developed through primary and/or secondary research. Write a formal outline of headings and subheadings before attempting to write a first draft of these sections.

2

Review of Literature

The most helpful sources were Coe (1992), Hammond (1982), and

Schele (1998). Written with Peter Mathews, Schele's book explains the

key elements of Maya writing and how they were discovered. Coe, an

archaeologist and epigrapher, discusses the contributions made to

Mayan epigraphy by scholars of the 20th century. Hammond, a British

archaeologist who worked in Belize, gives a good overview of Maya his-

tory and culture.

The GBonline web site provided information about Maya codices and

a timeline of the rise and fall of Maya civilization. David Stuart's online

article (1996) is a comprehensive decoding of the history of the Maya

rulers of Copan found in the glyphs on Altar Q.

Box 3.9: Review of Literature

Having such an outline will speed up your work and help you organize the content logically. It is much easier to write an organized, complete report draft from an outline and a set of research notes than it is developing a text directly on your word processor. The longer your report, the more levels of organization you will need in your headings, as discussed in Chapter 1.

Each section should describe completely a specific aspect or phase of your investigation. Use short topic paragraphs to introduce each section, reminding the reader of its purpose and relationship to the overall goal. Summarize the section and indicate its importance in the final paragraph. Follow the guidelines discussed in Chapter 2 to write a clear, readable report.

Conclusion

Scientific reports and technical papers differ in their approach to conclusions.

Scientific reports describe field and lab methodology first, and then provide the data under a heading called "Results." They present data in one or more tables, with the text describing the important features. The analysis of the data appears under a heading called "Discussion." This section analyzes the data sets and often includes charts, graphs, or other visual elements.

In science, the heading "Conclusion" suggests a new scientific principle or discovery arising from the experimental data. However, for technical readers, this heading usually indicates only a summary and preliminary analysis of field or lab data.

College students write most term papers entirely from secondary research. Their purpose is to summarize information and ideas from the published works of recognized authorities in a clear, readable form and to document these sources thoroughly. Therefore, the conclusion section in a term paper is shorter and less emphatic than in a technical report that analyzes lab work or field work. The conclusion of a term paper reflects on the content by summarizing the most important ideas and applying them to the central question or purpose stated in the introduction. It may also reflect the writer's own thoughts or ideas, stated clearly and concisely.

References (List of References, Literature Cited, or References Cited)

The list of references is a separate element. Place it on a new page, which should be the last numbered page in your report. Put the title in bold capital letters centred at the top. Choose the heading that is appropriate for your list of published sources, according to the documentation system you are using.

13

CONCLUSION

The development of Maya writing closely parallels the development of Maya civilization. A good example is the shift in the early Classic period from the written forms used for the codices to the forms used on permanent monuments.

Sir Eric Thompson made the first translations of Maya glyphs, but these were few and led to misconceptions about Maya civilization as a passive culture of priests and astronomers. Tatiana Proskouriakoff found an important key in the use of name and city glyphs within Mayan "cartouches." She was thus able to translate most of the monument glyphs at Tikal and Palenque. These proved to be written histories of their warrior kings. Linda Schele extended Proskouriakoff's work to include the codices and many stelae.

Box 3.10: Conclusion

A "Literature Cited," "References Cited," or "Works Cited" list consists of only those published works that you have paraphrased or quoted directly in the report body, using the correct form of citation.

A "List of References" or "References" list includes more than those published works that you have paraphrased or quoted directly; it also includes uncited sources. This type of material usually consists of general reference works such as dictionaries, encyclopedias, taxonomies of species, and textbooks. A student writer will typically use these in the early phases of research to focus the investigation and select appropriate topic areas for further study. In some cases, the writer may need to understand scientific or technical principles, processes, and practices that underlie the subject of investigation. These background sources of information may be included in this broader list for readers who are likely to want more information than just the cited sources.

Reference lists are single-spaced with hanging indentation. Chapter 5 provides a complete description and examples of text citations and reference lists.

Glossary

Write a glossary if you have used a large number of scientific and technical terms in the text of your report. Write a definition for each term in simple language and provide appropriate examples. List the terms in alphabetical order.

The glossary may also be placed in the front matter after the illustrations page.

Shorter reports typically contain only five or six terms that your reader may not know. In this case, write clear definitions for these in the text when you first introduce the term and omit the glossary from your report.

Appendix

An appendix is a separate element placed at the end of the report. It contains materials that support the descriptions in the text but are not required in the text. The decision about where to place supporting materials is up to you as the writer. In general, you should include supporting materials within the text of the report when such material is useful or essential to the reader's understanding of the written description. All other materials belong in an appendix. If these materials are varied, several separate appendixes may be appropriate.

Appendix materials may include field or journal notes, tables of raw field or lab data, graphic material such as sketch maps or seismograms, photograph or satellite image series, or copies of correspondence or other supporting documents.

Add a new page immediately following the reference list with the single word "APPENDIX" centred in bold capital letters. Do not number pages in a short appendix.

For appendixes longer than 10 pages, add a Table of Contents immediately following the "APPENDIX" title page. Group related types of supporting materials, such as photos or computer source code, in separate appendixes. Place a bold, capitalized heading centred at the top of the first page of each new appendix. Identify your appendixes or groups of appendixes with capital letters in sequence: "APPENDIX A," "APPENDIX B," and so on.

3.4 USE OF TABLES AND FIGURES

Write with pictures. There are two types of report graphics: tables and figures. Use tables for raw data from your field and lab work. Use figures to summarize data and to show data trends. Your reader depends on graphics for the key information in your report. Learn the strengths and weaknesses of each form of graphic communication. Graphic literacy is as important to the scientific and technical writer as language literacy.

Graphic Placement

Choose your graphics carefully. Is the graphic information important to your reader? Does it accomplish your purpose? If the answer is yes, include the graphic in your report. If not, omit it. A scientific or technical report is no place for graphic ornamentation.

If you have you written a description of methods, instrumentation, or results, consider adding a table or figure to summarize data or to improve your reader's understanding of processes. If possible, place these graphics on the same page as your written descriptions.

Do you have tables or figures associated with the subject of your report but not discussed directly in your text? Examples of this kind of information include tables of daily instrument readings, satellite photographs of study areas, or schematics of instrument circuits. If so, place these graphics in your report appendix.

Graphic Integration with Text

Integrate your graphics with the text. You must make good decisions about where to introduce your reader to a graphic in the flow of your description and analysis of work. You must also write text that will support the graphic by explaining its detail and its importance in your report's findings. Without integration, your reader will lose meaning; your text will be harder to understand without the graphic, and the graphic will lose its importance without the context of your discussion. Do not stuff all your graphics in an appendix because you are not sure what else to do with them. Deliver graphics to your reader at the right spot in your report.

Place a graphic immediately following the first text passage that discusses the information or idea shown in the graphic. Refer the reader to the graphic with a textual reference in parentheses, like this: (see Figure 1). Figure 1 should follow immediately on the same page or, if it is a large graphic, on the following page. Use the correct wrapping commands in your word processing software to wrap text around the graphic. You may discuss aspects of this graphic in later sections of your report. It is easier for your reader to refer back to a graphic already introduced than to imagine one not yet seen.

Tables

Table Number and Title

Access to information is essential in a report. The following rules allow your reader easy access to the tables in your report.

Figure 1. Frequency Distribution of Ceramics at El Pilar by Maya Period (Wernecke, 1993)

Period	Frequency	Percentage
Preclassic	4	1.5
Middle Preclassic	1	0.4
Late Preclassic	10	3.8
Early Classic	26	9.8
Late Classic	65	24.2
Terminal Classic	1	0.4
Indeterminate	158	59.8
Total	264	100.0

Box 3.11: Table Format

Give each table a table number and a descriptive title. Place these *above* the table. Use Arabic numerals for table numbers. Number your tables in sequence from the beginning of your text. List each table number and title on your illustrations page opposite the table's page number.

Begin the title block for the table at the left margin, single-spaced. You may add short sentences of explanation after the title. If the units of measurement are the same for all data, add them in parentheses after the title block. If you borrowed the data in the table from a secondary source, place an appropriate citation at the end of the title block. For more information on citations, consult Chapter 5.

Table Format

Separate the title block from the vertical column headings with a heavy line or a light double line. Separate the vertical column headings from the data with a light line. If text or footnote follows the table on the same page, separate the table from these lines of text with a line. Do not enclose a table with a border.

Notice in the example that footnotes explain data parameters. Do not use footnotes in the text of your report, only in tables.

You can import a table created in a spreadsheet program into your word processor or set one up from scratch by setting table columns directly on the page using appropriate tab stops. The finished table must have the correct scientific format. Do not divide columns and rows with lines.

Normal format for tables is "portrait," that is, with the long side of the printed page at the sides. You can print tables too wide for portrait printing in a landscape format, with the long sides of the page at the top and bottom. Landscape tables must be rotated 90° to the left, leaving the bottom of the table at the right-hand margin of the page.

For another example of a table, see the student report in Appendix E.

Figures

Figures Number and Title

Give each figure a figure number and a descriptive title. Place these *below* the figure. Use Arabic numerals for figure numbers. Number figures in sequence from the beginning of your text. List each figure number and title on your illustrations page opposite the corresponding page number.

Begin the figure number and title at the left margin of the page, single-spaced. You may add short sentences of explanation after the title. If you have borrowed the figure or the data in the figure from a secondary source, place an appropriate citation at the end of the title block. For the correct forms of citations, see the Chapter 5.

Figure Format

Place large figures on separate, numbered pages immediately following the first reference to them in the report text. Place smaller figures on the same page as text, using the text wrap features of your word processing software. In those cases, begin the title block at the left margin of the figure itself. For more information on text wrapping and figure formatting in Microsoft Word, see Appendix D.

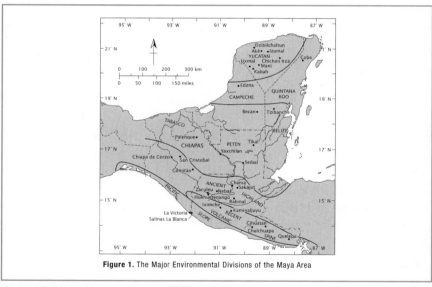

Figure 1. The Major Environmental Divisions of the Maya Area

Box 3.12: Figure Format

CHECKLIST FOR REPORT FORMAT

During your report formatting stage, be sure that you have done the following:

- Separated reports, inferences, and judgments into different sections of your report.
- Formatted your letter correctly, with a heading, inside address, salutation, body, and a complimentary close.
- Composed your letter to deal directly with one issue.
- Made your letter paragraphs short and sequenced correctly, with the purpose stated first, business details discussed second, action required specified last.
- In your memo, covered a single topic.
- Formatted your memo correctly, with correct guidewords and single-spaced paragraphs.
- Written a descriptive subject line for your e-mail.
- Sent your e-mail only to those who need the information.
- Proofread your e-mail carefully.
- Checked your report's spacing and margin, typefaces, headings, and page numbering.
- Decided how to present your report—stapled, in an envelope, in report covers, or spiral bound.
- Checked the content and form of each formal element—title page, table of contents, list of illustrations, abstract, body, reference list, glossary, appendix.
- Chosen graphics that communicate essential information to the reader and made sure that they placed in the best possible location in your report and are properly integrated with your text.

Chapter

Types of Reports

4

Overview: This chapter describes nine important types of workplace documents: instructions and manuals, progress reports, field trip reports, research reports, incident reports, inspection reports, proposals, feasibility reports, and government reports.

4.1 INSTRUCTIONS AND MANUALS

A set of instructions is a common type of technical document, along with its longer form, the manual. You will write instructions for the operator, someone who will be doing the procedure you describe. The purpose of writing instructions is to allow the operator to perform the procedure successfully.

Instructions vary in length from a single sheet to a dozen pages or more. You can also include them as sections within a longer scientific or technical report. In either case, good instructions explain the proper steps in operating equipment accurately and safely or in performing lab or field tests.

Keys to Successful Instructions

You will find that writing instructions for others about scientific and technical procedures that you know can be both satisfying and frustrating. Passing along your expertise to other people satisfies professional and personal needs. However, technicians often find writing difficult. Words and illustrations in a set of instructions must appear in just the right combinations to produce a reasonable chance of the operator's being able to perform the procedure successfully. Before you write, keep in mind the following simple keys to writing a successful set of instructions:

- *Keep it simple.* Wordy descriptions and elaborate examples prevent the reader from seeing clearly what to do next. Get directly to the appropriate actions.

- *Know the procedure.* If you are not completely familiar with all the steps, consult people who have the information you need.
- *Put yourself in the reader's place.* Most readers of technical instructions have some familiarity with basic principles and practices, but some do not. It is always better to give complete information to the operator than to assume that he or she knows what to do. Remember how it felt to ride a bike for the first time? Your reader will feel awkward and uncomfortable the first two or three times through the procedure. Provide content that will direct him or her to a successful completion. For example, include tests to determine whether the procedure was indeed successful.
- *Visualize the procedure in detail.* After visualizing it for yourself, choose illustrations that will show your reader clearly how to perform each step and demonstrate what the outcome of that step should look like.
- *Test your instructions on readers.* No matter how well you express, organize, and support your descriptions with examples in a set of instructions, there are bound to be omissions and areas that are not clear. Ask a variety of people—especially those who might actually be using your instructions—to read your document and, if possible, to perform the procedure described. Their reactions will provide valuable feedback about sections in your instructions that require more explanation or an additional diagram.

When writing instructions, consider your audience. Their level of expertise is critical to the success of your instructions. It is easy for a scientist or technician to forget his or her own level of expertise and assume that the operator knows how to do simple subroutines. Never assume that the operator who reads your instructions will know how to do something. When in doubt, write it out.

Organizing Your Instructions

Studies of technicians who have to read and follow written instructions show that they typically do so after they have begun the procedure and run into trouble. It is often said, "If all else fails, read the manual." This means that the operator who reads your instructions will often be in trouble in the middle of the procedure, scanning for the right information to help him or her out of a jam. Therefore, you must organize your instruction steps in a logical sequence under descriptive headings so that your reader can easily find the steps that are a problem.

To organize your instructions, group the steps in the procedure into three or four general tasks, each with a common outcome. Explain the outcome and list the steps involved in that task. Such an overview gives your reader a clear idea of the expected result of each task and lets him or her know when the steps have achieved their goal.

Tools, instruments, and materials are essential to proper performance of a procedure. Be sure that each section of your instructions begins with a description of these so that the operator knows what to gather together before beginning the task. If instruments are complex, such as spectrophotometers or magnetometers, describe and illustrate the controls, their function, and their proper calibration. If this description is several pages long, give it a separate major heading.

Common tasks found in sets of instructions include the following:

- unpacking and setup
- installing and customizing
- basic operating
- routine maintenance
- troubleshooting.

Write your instructions in chronological order as they are normally performed. As you perform the procedure yourself, write detailed notes to keep the steps in the correct order. Keeping such notes will also allow you to anticipate operator errors and help you identify steps that need more explanation or detail, must be illustrated with photographs or diagrams, or require the operator to choose between routines within the procedure. If there are different routines possible, your instructions must describe the criteria for making the correct choice.

Safety Messages

When organizing the content of a set of instructions, always note procedures that have a safety concern. Then include appropriate safety messages in the text at a point where the operator is likely to read them before attempting the procedure. Safety messages are essential in any instructions describing procedures that might cause harm to the operator or the equipment being used. Standard safety messages are classified into three levels of urgency:

- *Danger*: an immediate threat to the operator, such as the use of a chainsaw.
- *Warning*: a potential threat to the operator if the equipment is used improperly.
- *Caution*: potential damage to the equipment if it is used improperly.

Safety messages must be easy to see. Set them apart from the text by leaving a blank line before and after the message. Use a bold heading to identify which type of safety message you are presenting, such as the following:

> WARNING
> *Move the power switch on the thinning saw to the "Off" position and apply the brake before attempting to sharpen or change the saw blade.*

Safety messages must be easy to read. Message text written in jargon or technical terminology cannot be understood by every operator and can lead to serious injury. Recent lawsuits have led insurance companies to require their insured clients to maximize readability levels for safety messages and instructions in their products. Define your terms clearly and write your message in the clearest, most direct language possible.

Place the safety message *before* your description of the steps that are potentially hazardous. This placement will increase the likelihood that the operator will have read and understood the message before attempting such steps and will avoid injury or damage to the equipment.

Content of Instructions

Introduction

The introduction to your instructions needs to include the overall purpose of the procedure. Describe the main tasks and how they contribute to the final outcome. If the procedure is based on a scientific principle or theory of instrument operation, describe these briefly. An operator who understands clearly the goal of the procedure and its basic theory is more likely to perform the procedure successfully.

The introduction also includes any training that the operator requires to perform the procedure properly, such as any necessary safety instruction and any preparation of the work area. In a bulleted list, enumerate all the tools, instruments, and materials that the operator needs.

Include any other background information that an operator might require, such as a study area map or emergency contact information.

Procedures

Group all the steps in the procedure into a simple sequence of tasks. Give each task a descriptive heading. Number the steps in sequence under each task heading. Keep your description of each step simple. Focus on single, completed actions. Where the operator must make a choice between procedures, list the options first and describe clearly the criteria by which the operator must make the choice.

State your instructions in the imperative mood; for example, "Turn the edge clamp into place with the Allen key." Do not use the passive voice, as in "The edge clamp is turned into place with the Allen key." Except in short, one-page informal instructions, do not use recipe style that drops English articles, such as "Turn edge clamp into place with Allen key."

Integrate your illustrations carefully with the text. Good graphics are essential to the success of a set of instructions. Place appropriate graphics on pages with steps that require illustration. Wrap your text around small graphics and set larger ones immediately above the steps that they illustrate; show the picture and then describe.

Conclusion

Conclude with necessary reminders to the operator, such as the following:

- maintenance tips and schedules
- troubleshooting checklists
- steps to test the success of the procedure.

If your instructions are part of a longer report, write a short section summarizing how the procedure effectively achieves its goal and linking the procedure to the next major topic in the report.

Manuals

Write manuals using generally the same format and structure as you would use for instructions. Manuals are longer and include descriptions of instruments and complex processes that require more detail. They represent a greater investment of the writer's time and the company's resources. Manuals are usually collaborative efforts of people with specific expertise in writing and in scientific and technical procedures. The need for clearly written manuals is urgent because of competitive markets and the complexity of modern instrumentation. A good scientist or technician who can also write well is a valuable asset to a company producing technical manuals.

Manuals have multiple audiences: operators, consulting engineers and technicians, corporate buyers, and repair technicians. They also have multiple purposes: step-by-step instruction, explaining operating principles, and reassuring the user. These multiple audiences and purposes require multiple approaches to writing in different sections of the manual. They also necessitate writing in the clearest possible English to appeal to a wide range of readers. Technical accuracy is essential in a manual. You will have to revise your text extensively and field test the procedures described in the manual to make sure you got them right.

In the manual's front matter, write an overview of the contents and explain to the reader how to use the manual effectively. Identify typical users of this particular manual, the components of the products it describes, and the purpose of the procedures presented. Organize your content under logical, descriptive headings and lay out this plan for the reader in the introduction. Each reader of a manual is interested in only the specific sections that meet his or her needs. Therefore, organize and label clearly all sections of your manual.

Divide the content of a manual into labelled sections. Write in a clear, formal style and provide detailed illustrations. Suit your content to specific audiences, such as diagnostic tests to check the operation of instrument assemblies for a field technician, and choose patterns of organization to suit your content.

Conclude a manual with necessary reference material for the user: a glossary listing alphabetically all scientific and technical terms, an index listing alphabetically all keywords and headings by page number, and/or an appendix with data sets presented in appropriate ways, such as graphs, reference charts, maps, or test checklists.

4.2 PROGRESS REPORTS

You will write progress reports as a project supervisor, usually for a middle manager. The manager, in turn, may summarize a number of project progress reports in a monthly brief to senior management and may pass along progress reports to a client who is paying for the contract. The purpose of the progress report is to update management and/or clients on project tasks completed and those that still remain.

Managers need the information in your progress report to record your project's operational details, to evaluate it, and to account for the time and money you spent on the work. Regular progress reports allow managers to make mid-project decisions: to adjust timetables, re-allocate budgets, or reschedule the delivery of supplies and equipment. They allow you to provide your manager with current information on the project and with options for dealing with unanticipated technical problems and costs.

Full, detailed progress reports meet senior management's needs for planning immediate and future company projects and for completing current projects on time and on budget.

Progress reports also meet the project supervisor's needs to fulfill his or her duties on the current project. These duties include writing progress reports and keeping company management informed as the project moves forward. Fulfilling project duties in a timely and efficient manner is career development for the project supervisor. Good progress reports also allow the supervisor to write better completion reports at the end of each project and to write them efficiently. The form of the completion report is similar to that of the progress report. Its detail is mostly a summary of the information already set out in progress reports, and its evaluation of the project comes from the detailed knowledge of the technical problems and solutions encountered on the project that were described in the project's progress reports.

Progress Report Schedule

The schedule for reporting comes from the circumstances of the project. The manager responsible for the project will assign reporting duties to the project supervisor. If the project has been undertaken as contract work for a client company or a government agency, the contract will spell out a timeline for the project that includes a progress report schedule.

Reports are usually required at specified time intervals: weekly, biweekly, monthly, and so on. Progress reports can also be required at the completion of major tasks or stages of the project identified in the project timeline.

For smaller projects, progress reports can be less formal; for example, a client or a manager responsible for the project may request a progress report from time to time. The project supervisor may decide to submit a progress report when unusual or unforeseen circumstances arise on the job.

Progress Report Format

Write progress reports on small projects as letters if you are addressing them to clients and as memos if you are writing for a project manager within the company. Larger projects involving longer periods, more detailed work, and more company resources require more formal report formats, either short or long, depending on the amount of scientific and technical information in the report and the number of formal elements required to provide the reader with easy access to the data.

Write all progress reports for the project in the same format and pattern of organizing information. Consistency ensures the availability of uniform, complete data at the end of the project so that its successes and failures can be properly evaluated. It is also easier for your audience to read successive reports if they all appear in the same format.

Tips for Progress Reports

Gather the information you need for your report. Remember that a progress report looks back at what you have accomplished and forward at what is to come. Report your activities on the project over the applicable reporting period. Check your information for completeness and accuracy. Then forecast your activities on the project for the next reporting period. Focus on work that you and your staff have planned and on solutions that you intend to apply to current problems.

The basics of a progress report consist of time, tasks, and topics. Organize your descriptions of work completed and planned in chronological order, the order of events. Divide the steps completed and planned into tasks, the allocation of the work effort. Any problems encountered or evaluations of progress are special topics that need to be set aside in separate sections.

A project supervisor needs to keep good records. A daily log or journal of events and a file of paperwork containing letters, memos, invoices, and so on will provide the complete, accurate, detailed information you require to prepare a progress report and the completion report at the end of the project.

Parts of the Progress Report

Below is a general description of the elements of a typical progress report, as well as their sequence. Each reporting situation has its own needs and variations on the basic requirements for information. Adapt the format shown here to individual college or work situations by adding to, omitting from, or re-ordering the topic list.

Note that an executive summary is often included. Write one if you are submitting the progress report to management. Typically, an executive summary is placed after the front matter and before the formal introduction to the report.

- *Introduction.* Describe the scope and purpose of your project. If your project is a result of a successful proposal, check that document for the goals and scope of the proposed work. These statements of goals and limits for project work are important because they direct onsite decisions about allocating resources. Each progress report should restate the goals of the project clearly. Sometimes you will have to alter the goals in the middle of the project because of delays or technical problems. Describe any such changes to the scope and purpose of the project so that your reader can compare the original plan with the revised one. Include the dates for the reporting period covered by the report and the major stages of the project completed up to the date of the progress report.
- *Work Completed.* In this section, describe all the tasks completed on the job in the reporting period. Explain in steps how you accomplished the work. Group long step sequences under descriptive topic headings. For each main task, record the completion date. Include in this section any costs not in the project budget. Describe and explain any equipment or personnel changes that you made. Above all, describe and explain any problems or delays that occurred on the project. These are important to the manager who reads your report. However, do not include minor irritations that have no effect on the project timeline or budget. Summarize major problems that do affect the project. Leave a full description of your difficulties, with some options for a solution, to a separate section dealing with problems and adjustments. If you had no problems and all is well on your project, say so.
- *Work Remaining.* Describe the tasks that you have planned for the next reporting period. Give details of the tasks that you feel you can reasonably complete within that period. Be realistic in your estimates. On-the-job experience will help you here. When reporting your work planning, you may find yourself wanting to estimate more work done in less time in order to impress your reader, often your boss. Keep in mind that a manager is more impressed by conservative

estimates with a high probability of completion than by inflated expectations that result in disappointment. Conclude this section by summarizing all tasks remaining on the project after the next reporting period and estimating the expected completion dates.

- *Problems and Adjustments.* Do not include this section in your progress report if you have not experienced problems or delays and do not plan any changes to the work schedule. However, most scientists and technicians know Murphy's Law: if something can go wrong, it will. Most projects will develop some sort of a serious problem that requires either solving or avoiding by changing the project goals. If misfortune strikes your project, describe in this section the problem and any efforts you made to solve it. Explain any changes that you are either recommending or implementing to the original schedule, scope and purpose, specific tasks, or cost estimates. Include only major obstacles in your report, those that impact the project's goals; do not describe minor irritations.
- *Conclusion.* Summarize the status of your project in terms of time and budget. Evaluate your progress to date in terms of the relative ease with which you have reached some of the project's objectives. Forecast future progress. Answer management's key questions: Are we on schedule? Are we on budget? Are there any major problems arising? Recommend changes to planned tasks, costs, and scheduling as needed.

Issues in Writing the Progress Report

Avoid generalities. If you have made little progress, say so. Be clear, short, direct, and factual. Do not pad the report.

Select information carefully. Remind your reader of the project's primary purpose and any secondary goals. Then include only details of events that promoted or delayed the successful completion of the project's goals. In scientific and technical projects, do not present partial data. Preliminary results can be misleading.

Remember to illustrate your text with appropriate graphs, charts, photographs, and so on to show your progress toward the project's goals over time. These will lend authority to your conclusions and any recommendations you have made.

What does progress mean? Think about this question because it will determine which details to include in your report. Progress can certainly mean completion of a specific phase of the planned work. It can also mean completion of preparation steps for the planned work: development of procedures for sampling or testing, ordering equipment, negotiating with suppliers, or briefing project personnel on required equipment or procedures.

However, progress can also mean failure. We learn more through our mistakes than we do through our successes. When something goes wrong on the project, as it inevitably does, we learn. We adapt. We persist. We overcome. Interim failure leads to results.

4.3 FIELD TRIP REPORTS

A field trip report records the process and the results of extensive field investigations, often in remote areas of Canada, particularly in industries associated with natural resources and environmental science and engineering. The audience for the field trip report is usually the investigator's immediate supervisor. Because this type of report contains detailed information and scientific data, it usually appears in formal technical report format, with all major elements of front and back matter.

Taking Good Field Notes

You can collect data on field data sheets instead of or in addition to using a field notebook. Begin each sheet with a statement of purpose, for example "to assess the habitat suitability of an area for intertidal organisms." Include base data with each inspection: date, location, field personnel, and weather conditions. A field data sheet should list any photographs or field samples collected.

The purpose of field work is to make observations and/or conduct experiments. The field notebook is often the only item brought back from the field, the sole permanent and original record of your work. Choose a compact, waterproof design. Quad paper is useful for sketching. The binding should be permanent; do not choose detachable pages. Never remove pages from a field notebook. Use a soft pencil for field work; graphite will not run or fail to work on damp paper. For lab work, use a pen with permanent ink.

Use the SCAN system for taking notes in the field. Field notes should be

- specific—quantify your observations.
- complete—note all significant detail.
- accurate—check your measurements and field identifications.
- neat—print or sketch clearly.

In addition to data required, record any questions or speculations that occur to you. Field work will stimulate your thinking about problems or situations you are observing. Write down questions, insights, intuitions, or possible connections between observed events. These will give you issues to think over later when writing up the report. Always keep data and analysis separate in your notebook. Use a code, such as underlining or square brackets, to identify insights or issues and separate them from observed data. Always interrupt recording data to write down analysis and capture ideas as they occur to you. Include sketches where appropriate.

Complete data in a field notebook should include the following:

- location—written detail and a sketched map so that others can locate the area
- purpose—questions asked and information sought
- method—steps taken and procedures followed, including modifications required
- tools—devices used to gather information
- results—measurements and record, of samples or photographs
- incidental observations—unplanned events or problems encountered.

Parts of the Field Trip Report

Divide the introduction to your field trip report into the following sections:

- *Aims.* Describe the primary goals of the field work and any secondary goals. Use action words, such as "to observe conditions," "to collect specimens," "to map soil types and forest cover," or "to measure water parameters."
- *Methods.* Describe the field techniques you used (for example, electrofishing), the instrumentation you used, and any modifications you made to the field method or instruments to suit conditions as you found them.
- *Field Trip Study Area.* Make at least a sketched map to orient your reader. In most cases, more serious cartography is required. Use a base map series, such as NTS or OBM, and add your own data sets relevant to the project. In the text of this section, describe the general location and topography of the area where you conducted the field study.

- *Background Data.* Include the following information about the field work: personnel in the crew; places, dates, times; and equipment and transportation required. When you have to brief or instruct a field crew, such as a tree planting crew, include the preparation of tools, materials, and the plant site in this section. Include also any previous research on the scientific or technical subject that you are investigating in the field. Indicate the general weather conditions during the field work, since these can affect the efficiency of the work and the data itself.

Keep good notes while in the field; they are the source of data for your report. In the body of the report, present your field activities in an organized fashion. Group similar activities or information under descriptive headings; for example, put geomorphology in one section and geophysical data in another. Use brief headings that encapsulate the topic instead of complete sentences or questions.

Avoid using chronological order for your report wherever possible. The sequence of when events happened is generally less important than the types of activities undertaken and the types of results obtained from the investigations. For example, a magnetometer survey yields data best presented to your reader on a map of rock formations, which are then described and interpreted in your text; the actual process of running grid lines with the magnetometer is not important to the reader.

Describe activities thoroughly and accurately. Choose only activities and events that are useful to your audience and suit your purpose. Field trips can be fun, but you must avoid personal anecdotes in your report. Present your field data in the form of appropriate tables and figures, as well as digital photographs, to illustrate and verify field conditions, natural processes, or technical procedures. Leave analysis of data to the end of the report.

Make sure you define scientific or technical terms used in your field trip report. Be concise. Edit your text carefully and eliminate unnecessary detail and vague generalizations.

Concluding the Field Trip Report

Include the following sections in your conclusion:

- *Summary.* Review your most important activities. Include the most significant results.

- *Results.* Analyze your data. Use tables and figures. Evaluate the success of your trip. Compare your reported results with the trip's goals.
- *Appendix.* Attach at least your field notes; these are necessary as they allow the reader to check the accuracy of the data presented in the body of the report.

4.4 RESEARCH REPORTS

We answer questions about natural processes by experimentation and by looking in scientific literature for reports of experiments that answer similar research questions. When you write up the results of your own experimental work, you are contributing to that body of scientific and technical literature.

The research report focuses on original work, called primary research. A report section called the review of literature, usually presented as part of the introduction, is the only secondary research found in this type of report. This section summarizes published reports dealing with similar investigations and information. The majority of the report text describes the purpose, methods, and results of your own scientific or technical research. It concludes with a discussion of the experimental results: a preliminary analysis, a summary of important details, and comparison of results with research goals.

Experts write research reports for other experts. When you read others' research reports, such as the report included in Appendix E, their content may not interest you because they are not in your field of study, but it is important to note that their organization and format are universal and therefore useful to you as you hone your writing skills. Keep in mind that readers of scientific and technical literature share specific interests and expertise with the writer. The goal of writing a research report is to inform those expert readers, not to interest, educate, or entertain them.

Parts of the Research Report

Divide the body of your research report into the sections described below. Note that you can also use this sequence of topics for articles describing your research that are written for publication in scientific and technical journals. If you are writing for publication, follow the format guidelines provided by the journal and its editorial staff.

- *Introduction.* Describe the general subject area of the investigation, the specific research goals, and the scope of the research, both as planned and as experienced. You can state your research goals in the form of a hypothesis, as a question to be answered, or as a simple statement of what was studied.

- *Review of Literature.* Include a review of literature that describes reports of previous research designed to answer similar questions. In college, write an extensive review to demonstrate a comprehensive knowledge of published literature in your research field. Make it a separate section with its own heading. In the workplace, describe only papers that helped you limit and focus your research project or identify effective methods or instrumentation. Include the review as a section within the introduction to your research paper.

- *Materials and Methods.* In this section, describe the design of your research project, including scientific and/or technical procedures used, as well as the materials, instrumentation, and other facilities used in the project. Your goal is to describe the experiment clearly enough that your reader could set up and run the same experiment with similar results.

- *Results.* This is the most important section in your report. It answers the questions in your statement of research purpose. Present the raw data from your observations and your measurements in the form of tables and figures. Point out the significant features and trends in the data.

- *Discussion.* Provide some interpretation of your results. Evaluate the results in terms of whether the investigation met the research objectives, state any problems with the methods or results, discuss inferences that you can draw from the data, and list implications for further research in the same area.

4.5 INCIDENT REPORTS

In every workplace, the unexpected occurs frequently. Whenever there is any deviation from normal operations—a serious malfunction, cost overrun, accident, production slowdown, personnel problem, breakdown of machinery, or any other unforeseen, unfortunate occurrence—you may be required to write an incident report for your supervisors.

Also called occurrence reports or accident reports, such reports are common in health and community development professions and in security and law enforcement. Professionals in science and technology also rely on them at budget time when the incident affects company finances, as parts of proposals to improve technical procedures, or as legal evidence.

Companies often require incident reports in a standard format that appears on a data sheet so that managers can review and compare information about incidents over time.

Process for Writing Incident Reports

First, investigate the incident at the site, then write the report based on your findings. Your report must describe the event that occurred, how it happened, what consequences it had, what were its possible causes, and what the response was, if any, that people made to the incident. Your supervisor may also ask you to recommend steps for preventing a similar incident in the future.

Begin the report by asking the journalists' questions: who, what, where, when, and how. The answers to these questions come from carefully observing the site and circumstances. They give you the factual details of the incident.

Make a judgment about the cause of the incident based on the details you have uncovered and the valid inferences you can draw. You might review the section on reports, inferences, and judgments in this book. Your judgment will determine whether any person or process is the cause of the incident.

In the concluding section, make recommendations about what your organization should do in the future to respond to a similar situation and to avoid similar incidents.

Write short incident reports in memo or e-mail format; format reports describing longer, more complex incidents in formal report style with formal elements. Remember to expand, subdivide, or modify the parts of the incident report to suit the amount of detail you uncover in your investigation.

Parts of the Incident Report

- *Introduction.* In your opening section, cover the topics listed below.

  - *Purpose.* Describe the reason for this report; for example, to inform a superior or department.

- *Scope.* Describe the limitations of the report; for example, say that descriptions are limited to the remote monitoring station malfunction that took place on a specific date and to a preliminary analysis of the causes.
- *Background.* Describe the circumstances leading up to the incident; for example, the purpose of new equipment and the date it was installed in the station.

- *Investigation.* This section is limited to the facts of the incident: what events happened and in what sequence. It should answer the questions of who, what, where, when, and how. Include exact date, time, and location. If staff members were involved in the incident, include their names, positions, and departments. If the incident resulted in personal injury, include the name, address, phone number, and employer of anyone who was involved but is not employed by your company. Include details of the physical location and circumstances such as the make and model of vehicles involved or a sketch map of the area or room where the incident occurred. If equipment was part of the incident, record the make and model, serial numbers, and other details as needed. Write these up in a simple, chronological narrative. Remember that more information is better. Sometimes small details found during the investigation can prove later to be significant pieces of evidence.
- *Causes.* Review the main events of the incident. Then draw inferences about possible causes, examining carefully the significant facts of the incident as noted in your investigation. This section answers the "why" question. Which person or group of people or process was the cause of the incident?
- *Results.* Describe the consequences of the incident: injuries to staff members or others, loss of equipment or production time, delays in normal operations, or extra costs. Include any responses that employees made immediately to the incident. In the case of injury, describe the extent of the injury and how it was treated after the incident occurred. When equipment was damaged or failed to function, describe how it was repaired or replaced and provide details of the associated costs in time and money.

- *Recommendations.* List your recommendations for the company, organization, or individual reader to help avoid a similar incident again. These must be practical, concrete suggestions. Provide them in a bulleted list or in short paragraphs. Recommend as much as your position and authority allow. Where further incidents are inevitable, include recommendations for appropriate responses to the situation. Where the incident investigation reveals multiple issues, make individual recommendations for each issue.

4.6 INSPECTION REPORTS

Inspection reports, also called service reports, focus on technologies: equipment, systems, or site installations. Routine inspections may uncover equipment failures, malfunctions, or accidental damage, or employees may report these types of technical problems as they occur during normal operations.

Inspections are as varied as technical occupations. An environmental technologist may be required to inspect monitoring stations for weather, stream pH, or seismic activity in remote locations. A civil engineering technologist may have to inspect construction work, such as that of a building, a road, or a bridge.

Do not be tempted to write the details in chronological order. Most readers of inspection reports are supervisors and want to know what happened, what impact the failure had, what caused it, and what steps will remediate the system. They don't want a detailed story about how the technician did the diagnostic testing or fixed the problem and got equipment back in operation.

Parts of the Inspection Report

- *Introduction.* In your opening section, cover the topics listed below.

    - *Purpose.* Describe the purpose of the inspection and say on whose authority it was performed. This second type of information is important when, for example, the technician must carry out the inspection on private property.
    - *Scope.* Describe the limitations of the inspection, including the area or equipment inspected.

- *Background.* List all circumstances of the inspection, including names and positions of staff assisting in the inspection, the date, and the location of the equipment or system. Include a sketch map of the area where necessary.
- *Investigation.* Describe steps taken to inspect the installation, system, or equipment. Indicate the general condition of operating equipment, including any failure or malfunction and how it manifested itself. Indicate any unacceptable conditions or missing parts. Include any specific technical problems you encountered that need solutions, as well as any work required to maintain or upgrade the system.
- *Causes.* Describe any specific diagnostic procedures undertaken to determine the cause of failure. Indicate the cause or causes when the diagnostic points clearly to one or more specific problems as the cause. If you cannot determine the cause or causes after inspection and running diagnostic tests, say so. Do not avoid addressing this issue.
- *Results.* Indicate the consequences of the failure, including any further technical or system problems and any changes required in operating procedures. Include your judgment on whether the failure was the result of a one-time problem or whether it is an infrequent or recurring problem. Your recommendations will flow from this judgment, since recurring failures will require more extensive and frequent maintenance and inspection of equipment, redesign of technologies, replacement of equipment or systems, or revised operating procedures. Estimate costs of the failure or malfunction. Your manager will need these to assess alternative solutions.
- *Recommendations.* If required, recommend options for improvement in operating procedures, equipment, or systems.

4.7 PROPOSALS

The purpose of writing a proposal is to describe a proposed plan of work that will solve a problem or improve a process and to get the reader to finance that proposed plan of work. North American corporations and governments routinely contract private sector work in this manner.

A second important purpose of a proposal is to get you and your company accepted to do the work. A good plan of work that solves scientific and technical problems is essential to a good proposal—but a good plan can be offered by other contractors, not just your company. Your proposal must also convince the reader that you and your company are best qualified to do the work.

Types of Proposals

Internal proposals are submitted within your company to supervisory staff. They are suggestions for new or improved processes and facilities. Their format is usually brief and informal. External proposals are submitted to clients outside your company and result in contracts that make money. Their format is longer, more detailed, and more formal in style.

Unsolicited proposals are submitted without a prior request for a proposal. Researching the market and networking with associates will help identify potential clients who would read an unsolicited proposal. Informal meetings with such clients will show you what their needs are and how to address them in the proposal.

Solicited proposals are submitted in response to a request from a potential client, often a government agency. These requests usually appear in two forms. An Information for Bid (IFB) is a request for standard products and services, such as cleaning or food services. A Request for Proposal (RFP) is a request for customized products or services. Most scientific and technical services, such as geological field surveys or the engineering of structures, fall into this second category.

Keys to Successful Proposals

Here are some tips on writing successful proposals.

- *Understand the client's problem or situation clearly.* This is the single most important factor in your proposal. Your understanding of the client's needs must be thorough and accurate. Do your homework on the client's situation, then use this understanding of the client's needs to write well-structured and well-expressed sections of your proposal. The client's recognition that you have understood his or her situation or problem is the key motivation in giving the contract to you and your company.
- *Write a practical, detailed plan of work.* The procedures you describe must be easy to achieve. They are usually standard processes with some modification to suit the client's needs. Provide enough detail to show your reader that you are familiar with the type of work being described.

- *Estimate a good price for the work.* The total value of the work need not be the lowest price possible. The client will weigh the costs of submitted proposals against other factors, such as the design of the work and the reliability of the company itself. However, your price must be competitive.
- *Provide the company's credentials.* If the other factors are all equal among competing companies, the contract will usually go to the company with the most experience. Therefore, include a section describing your company's previous projects and the qualifications of the principal staff members who will be responsible for the proposed work.

Proposals require more than good technical description—they require persuasive writing. Include sections that show how the future benefits of the project outweigh the costs. These sections must persuade that you understand the problem or opportunity exactly, that you have a detailed plan, and that company has the credentials to do the work.

Parts of a Proposal

For a solicited proposal, follow IFB or RFP guidelines exactly. These are usually published in some detail, including the nature and extent of the work, as well as format requirements for the proposal document itself. Look for key details in the language of the proposal. Scientific or technical words and phrases that are frequently repeated are clues to the essential concerns of the potential client. Address these concerns in detail in your proposal. When revising and editing the document, ensure that these keywords and phrases appear frequently. Such phrases found in government RFPs often represent the political agenda of the government in power and the areas where they are prepared to fund projects that meet their criteria.

The following sections outline the format for an unsolicited proposal. Since projects vary considerably, you will not need to cover all of the topics in equal detail. Be sure to consider each one carefully before deciding what to write. Then add, combine, reorganize, or omit topics to suit your proposal. Above all, research the project thoroughly. Good proposals are built on complete, accurate detail.

Summary

Provide a summary in either the front matter or the body of your report. Include in your summary all the major points in your proposal: the definition of the problem, the proposed program of work, your company's qualifications and experience, a timeline for work, and the budget estimates.

Introduction

Outline your subject and purpose. Describe what kind of work you will propose and what its outcome will be.

Describe the problem faced by the potential client, as you understand it. Write short, detailed paragraphs. Quantify each aspect of the problem wherever possible. Be accurate. Check your lab or field test measurements, as well as secondary source data.

Describe the current technologies that you intend to apply to this problem. Most readers of proposals are well educated but unfamiliar with specific technologies used in other fields. For example, describe the theory of operation of state-of-the-art equipment and support it with a simple diagram or flow chart.

Proposal Plan

Organize your proposed plan of work into sections and use subheadings that identify the major tasks to be accomplished. A clear structure of headings and subheadings makes it easier for the reader to absorb the detail and understand it. Be specific in your description of the steps in each task referring to your research notes to get the necessary details. Your description must be thorough, covering all aspects of the problem. It may include your own estimates and test measurements, as well as secondary research in current scientific and technical literature.

Check your facts and figures carefully. Mistakes in measurements undermine client confidence. During the revising stage, look for errors of expression specifically at those points where you are explaining principles and processes.

Avoid generalities. It is tempting in a proposal to shorten the work of writing by estimating quantities of materials or time required to complete the proposed work without the benefit of extensive experience or research. The clue to generality is the relative term. A statement such as "This process will take only a short time" will signal to the proposal reader that you do not have an exact estimate of the time required, since "short" is a relative term. In a proposal, you must commit to specifics wherever possible.

Avoid statements assuring the reader of your enthusiasm and competence. These mean little on paper, since anyone can say them without meaning them. What speaks most clearly to the reader about your enthusiasm and ability to do the proposed work is the work that you have already put into the proposal, both the research and the writing. An accurate, detailed, well-organized plan of work will show that you can and want to do the work.

Include appropriate illustrations to support the principles and processes in your proposed plan of work. Tables, diagrams, flow charts, cutaway views, photographs, and instrument layouts are some of the ways in which you can show the reader how the work would be done. Include also any estimates of costs that you have received from potential suppliers or subcontractors.

Qualifications

Describe how you and your company are qualified to do the work in the proposed plan. Identify each staff member who would work on the proposed project. Include a résumé for the designated supervisor and a paragraph for each of the others.

List the major projects that your company has completed. Potential clients will want to see what you have done for other companies or agencies. Provide brief descriptions of projects, illustrated with photographs, that are similar to the project for which you are writing a proposal. List also the equipment and facilities for the proposed project that the company owns.

Describe your company's management structures, including chain of command, local offices, facilities, and corporate partnerships. Build a picture in this section of a company ready and able to do the work.

Remember that experience wins. If the plans of work and the costs are roughly the same among competing bids, the contract will go to the company with the most experience.

Scope and Methodology

Describe precisely and realistically how much work you plan to do. Most readers of proposals will be concerned about potential time and cost overruns. Therefore, set reasonable limits on the proposed work.

Describe also how you will do the work, providing an overview of the tasks and steps necessary to achieve the goal. Explain briefly any scientific or technical procedures required to complete each task, keeping in mind that the client reading the proposal may not be familiar with your company's technologies.

Facilities, Personnel, and Duration

Use a bulleted list to set out the equipment and estimates of supplies required to complete the project. Include any equipment rentals or contracted services necessary.

List the names and positions of the company personnel who will work on the project. Include the names of contracted persons or companies required to complete the project.

Estimate the total time required for the project. Then provide a detailed schedule of tasks and procedures. If possible, present this in the form of a chart or table. Remember to be accurate and complete in your estimates. If you underestimate or overestimate the time required for the project and this schedule becomes part of the contract, the time factor will become a problem for both parties.

Budget

Set out the budget for the project in the form of a financial statement with standard line items and associated costs. Divide your project budget into direct and indirect costs.

Direct costs include salaries and benefits, travel costs, equipment purchases and rentals, contracted services, materials, and supplies. Research each of these thoroughly to provide accurate estimates.

Indirect costs, also called overhead, are the many costs associated with doing business. These include clerical services, utilities for offices and buildings, and maintenance of vehicles and facilities. Since these indirect costs are too numerous and too small to estimate individually, express them as a percentage of direct costs, usually about 10 percent for large projects up to 30 percent for smaller ones.

Reports and Benefits

Most projects of any length and complexity require the project manager to submit regular progress reports to his or her supervisor and to the client. Indicate in this section the personnel on the project responsible for writing progress reports, specify the reporting intervals, and spell out the form that the progress reports would take.

Most important, end with a section called "Benefits" that details the advantages of the project to the potential client. Begin by describing the outcomes of the proposed plan of work—that is, what the client will have when you are finished. Then identify the benefits to the client in terms of the problem or situation you described in the opening sections. Organize your list of benefits in more-to-less-important order. By placing the benefits section at the end of your proposal, you will leave your reader with a positive impression of the proposed plan of work and of your company.

Appendix

An appendix is not required but may be useful in providing a depth of detailed information that would not be appropriate in the body of the report. It can also include further testimonials to the company's credentials, a key element in any successful proposal. Items that can prove useful are letters or e-mails from satisfied clients, detailed task schedules presented as Gantt or milestone charts, and evaluations of previous projects from third parties, both qualitative and quantitative.

Researching and writing a good proposal takes time. In the end, your proposal may not win the contract, but a good proposal will always leave a positive impression and lead to better opportunities in the future for you and your company.

4.8 FEASIBILITY REPORTS

A feasibility report presents the results of a feasibility study, a series of investigations into whether a proposed plan of work is feasible or "do-able." Feasibility studies may consider a broad range of factors or only one or two—engineering and technical possibilities, economic practicalities, ecological balance, social values, or psychological health, for example. Feasibility studies that deal with large and complex issues involving science and technology usually assess the feasibility of two or more options for solving the central issue or problem.

Design the feasibility study itself to answer a clear and focused question. For example, "The purpose of this investigation is to recommend to the Forest Pest Management Institute the most appropriate method of forest pest control in the watershed of the Nashwaak River in New Brunswick." Investigating something out of scientific or technical curiosity does not constitute a feasibility study. Your purpose is to recommend something specific to someone specific.

Feasibility studies are often carried out in teams of experts, and thus the teams often write the reports that describe these studies. A good example is the environmental impact study. When a new highway is proposed, teams of civil engineers, fisheries and wildlife biologists, environmental technologists, geotechnical technologists, urban planners, and archaeologists study alternative routes for their environmental impact. Each contributes to the final feasibility report that recommends one proposed route over the other possibilities.

Parts of a Feasibility Report
Below are the standard components of a feasibility report.

- *Introduction.* Begin with the purpose and scope of the feasibility study. The amount of information collected during the course of the investigation will depend on time and resources, whatever the original goals. It is important to reveal to your reader how much data you were able to collect in order to answer the feasibility question stated in the purpose. Describe briefly the problem that you investigated and the methods you used to acquire information.
- *Discussion.* In this section, present the results of your investigations, organized into a logical sequence of subsections under descriptive headings. Illustrate your data sets with appropriate graphics, such as charts, graphs, photos, maps, histograms, and so on. Use the illustrations to interpret the results and draw appropriate inferences from the data.
- *Conclusions.* Summarize the data and review the purpose of the study. A vertical list is often the best way to present the most significant findings of a feasibility study.
- *Recommendations.* Make a bulleted list of recommended actions. Base each one on the conclusions developed directly from the data obtained from your investigations. Use the imperative mood; for example, "Apply BT in 300:1 concentrations to the spruce–jack pine component of the upper watershed forest stands." Remember that recommendations are your professional judgments; they are for your reader to consider and act on at his or her discretion.

4.9 GOVERNMENT REPORTS
Scientists and technologists working for federal, provincial, or municipal governments in Canada write reports explaining scientific and technical principles

and processes and applying them to current public problems and issues. The following outline provides an overview of the main elements present in a typical government report.

- *Introduction.* Include the official terms of reference for your study as set out by the authorizing government body, such as a planning council or policy review committee. Also include a review of the problem that you investigated, the public issue or issues that generated the research, and current approaches by other public governments. Describe in a section titled "Background" any history of the particular issue or problem that the report addresses.
- *Report Body.* Address one or more of the following issues, depending on your audience and on which issues are relevant to the problem that you are describing:
  - roles of public bodies
  - directions for improvement
  - concepts, principles, and information
  - feasibility
  - legal questions
  - public impact
  - policy and implementation issues
  - planning and resource issues
  - bylaw and statute conflicts and issues
  - evaluation processes.
- *Conclusion.* Finish the report with a summary of findings and recommendations if they are required by your terms of reference.
- *Front and Back Matter.* A government report is usually a formal report, requiring all the major elements. Front matter usually consists of a title page, letter of transmittal, table of contents, and an executive summary instead of an abstract. If the report has illustrations, provide a list of illustrations. The back matter includes a reference list, since you will likely refer in the report to scientific and technical literature and to Canadian statutes, and an appendix, since you will likely have supplemental material to support your text.

CHECKLIST FOR REPORT TYPES

Be sure that you have done the following:

Instructions and Manuals

- Familiarized yourself thoroughly with the procedure and followed research notes when writing.
- Kept it simple and put yourself in the reader's place.
- Tested your instructions on readers.
- Chose good illustrations.
- Provided an overview and a list of materials for each task.
- Checked whether safety messages were required and if so formatted them properly.
- Grouped instructions under headings.
- Used the imperative mood.
- Concluded with maintenance, troubleshooting, and/or testing.
- Divided your manual into chapters, as well as provided detailed overviews for your audience and included appendix reference material.

Progress Reports

- Understood who your reader is.
- Checked the progress report schedule.
- Used consistent format for all project reports.
- Gathered operational and planning information.
- Organized content into time, tasks, and topics.
- Answered management's key questions: Is the project on time and on budget? Any there any problems?

Field Trip Reports

- Took research notes from field study, using a data recorder or a notebook.
- Stated clearly in your introduction the aims and purpose of the field trip.

- Included a map of study area and background data.
- Organized content into similar activities or types of data, grouped under descriptive headings.
- Analyzed data with standard methodology.
- Presented your results with graphics.
- Included field notes in the appendix.

Research Reports

- Described research aims and goals in the introduction.
- Included a review of literature section to summarize and evaluate relevant published research.
- Included research design in the materials and methods section, with details about materials, instrumentation, and facilities.
- Presented your data in tables and figures, also describing and interpreting these in text.
- Double checked your data for accuracy.
- Revised and edited your report carefully.
- In the discussion section, evaluated the research plan, drawing inferences from data and listing implications for further research.

Incident Reports

- Investigated the incident thoroughly and wrote a complete set of notes at the time of the investigation.
- Wrote a strong introduction, with all the required parts.
- Described the incident completely, including all relevant details.
- Suggested the causes of the incident and described thoroughly the consequences of the incident.
- Made recommendations for improved procedures.

Inspection Reports

- Wrote a strong introduction, with all the required parts.
- Described the inspection completely, including all relevant details.

- Suggested the causes of any equipment malfunction and described thoroughly the consequences of any malfunction.
- Made recommendations for improved equipment design and operation.

Proposals

- Checked whether the proposal is solicited or unsolicited, and if the former, if it is a response to IFB or RFP.
- In the introduction, provided a practical, detailed plan of work, addressing client concerns completely and accurately.
- Checked your data.
- Described the technologies used.
- Kept your plan of work organized and logical sequenced and provided accurate information, including specific estimates.
- Described the company's qualifications, including personnel and previous projects.
- In the scope and methodology section, specified how much work would be done and in what way, describing practical limits and setting a timeline.
- Listed all equipment, supplies, and personnel required, as well as provided a timeline of main tasks with accurate estimates.
- In the budget section, included direct costs and indirect costs, with accurate estimates.
- Included a progress report schedule and specified the writer, audience, and format.
- Emphasized the benefits to the client and outcomes of proposed plan, organizing these in a more-to-less-important pattern.
- Considered whether an appendix is required and if so provided testimonials, detailed timelines, and/or details of company projects.

Feasibility Reports

- Included a clear statement of purpose of the feasibility study.
- If writing a team report, communicated effectively with team members and divided the writing jobs clearly.

- In the introduction, outlined the purpose, scope of investigations, and methods used.
- In the discussion, presented data and illustrated them.
- Organized content under descriptive headings.
- Provided an interpretation of main points.
- In the conclusion, included a summary and went over significant findings.
- Provided recommendations as a bulleted list of recommended actions.

Government Reports

- In the introduction, included official terms of reference and discussed the background.
- Addressed all the issues and organized them into a logical sequence under descriptive headings.
- Included all required front and back matter in the correct order.

Chapter

Report Documentation

5

Overview: This chapter sets out the correct format for documenting published sources of information used in scientific and technical reports. It also discusses ethical considerations in doing research work and reporting, including the issue of plagiarism.

5.1 ETHICAL CONSIDERATIONS

Søren Kierkegaard wrote, "One may ask even of a devotee of science that he should acquire an ethical understanding of himself before he devotes himself to scholarship, and that he should continue to understand himself ethically while immersed in his labours." To be a professional person is to have a code of ethics. Ethics is the practical application in daily life of a set of moral principles. A law defines minimum standards and is enforced by government. Ethics defines higher standards and is enforced by professional associations. These standards include the following:

1. rights—needs and welfare of individuals

2. justice—fair distribution of consequences within a group of an action or policy decision

3. utility—fair distribution of consequences on the general public of an action or policy decision.

In a conflict of standards, the higher principles are more important. Ethical problems have no precise resolutions because no rules can determine exactly which standards outweigh the others. This can frustrate engineers and technicians who are accustomed to precise, calculated solutions. Most people just do what they think is right, but the quality of their ethical decisions varies widely.

As an employee, you have obligations to your employer, to the public, and to the environment. To your employer, you owe proficiency and conscientiousness, ensuring that you have the proper training to do the work you've been asked to do and that you apply yourself thoroughly to that work. In addition, you owe your employer honesty, candour, confidentiality, and loyalty. Don't steal. Be truthful. Report potential problems before they become disasters. Most importantly for scientific and technical writers, do not falsify data presented to your employer in oral or written form. The results of field or lab research must be reported completely and honestly. Do not discuss company business with outside agencies. Act in your employer's best interest, not your own.

Your obligation to the public is principally to ensure that any product or service that your company offers is safe and conforms to accepted standards of functioning. The most common ethical principle applied in cases where a consumer has been injured is the "due care" principle. This principle affirms that the manufacturer knows more about the product than the consumer does and thus has more responsibility to ensure that the product or service complies with all its claims and is safe to use.

As a technical writer, you will often create documents for projects that have environmental implications. Alert your supervisor and work to reduce environmental impacts. If you are lucky enough to work in Canada's growing environmental sector, you may have the opportunity to promote environmental solutions directly, using your technical writing skills.

Trade secrets are confidential data owned by a company. You are obligated to protect your company's confidentiality. Fair use means providing accurate, not misleading, information about products or technologies, even if that means going over your supervisor's head. Avoid abstractions and generalities, jargon, and euphemisms.

Whistle-blowing is the act of going public with information about your company's unethical conduct. Knowing where your loyalty to your employer ends and your responsibility to the public begins is not easy. Whistle-blowing has severe consequences and should be a last resort. Consider first the following issues:

1. Get all the facts and be sure they are accurate. Incomplete information can lead to wrong conclusions.

2. Identify the ethical issue and ascertain who is being harmed.

3. Assess how serious the situation is. The more serious the problem, the more obliged you are to act.

4. Consider notifying the company's senior management instead of going public with your information. Think about the implications for yourself as well as for the public.

Codes of ethical conduct have become common in professional organizations in engineering and the sciences. Their purpose is to promote ethical behaviour among members. The Society for Technical Communication (STC) publishes "Ethical Guidelines for Technical Communicators"; these include legality, honesty, confidentiality, quality, fairness, and professionalism.

Ethics in Research

When conducting research projects involving other people, consider the following issues.

- Your research may require approval by an ethics review committee to ensure that you are not violating your college or company's code of ethics.
- Report your research results accurately. Describe what you observed or what you were told. Provide an overview of your research so that your discussion of specific data has a valid context.
- Respect property rights. Most types of research work require permission to access information or property. For example, although field research on Crown land does not require permission, research on private property requires the stated permission of the landowner.
- Avoid causing physical or emotional harm to people or damage to the environment.

Ethics also plays a major role when doing research online. Information on the Internet is often misidentified or misrepresented. Therefore, it is important for you to identify the source of information, the content, and the web site's structure and publisher. The following is a checklist of issues to address before deciding to use and document online information:

- *Accuracy.* It is the responsibility of the user to be aware of the information presented. Who published this site and is he or she qualified to do so?

  - Who is the author/editor/publisher of the web site? If no one is listed, perhaps the information is not accurate.

- Is the author affiliated with a known institution?
- Has the information been reviewed or edited by a third party?
- Is there a date listed for the creation (copyright) of the site or a date for the last update of the site?
- Is there a mail-to link to contact the author or the organization?
- Are references given for the use of statistics or facts?
- Does the writing follow the basic rules of grammar, spelling, and composition?
- Is a bibliography or reference list included?

- *Authority.* It is crucial to know whether the person, institution, or agency responsible for a site has the necessary qualifications and knowledge.

  - Is there an author listed for the page or the site?
  - Are the author's qualifications presented?
  - With whom is the author affiliated?
  - Is a publisher mentioned for the web site?
  - Does the publisher have a reputation?
  - Is contact information provided for the author or organization? Keep in mind that this does not necessarily indicate authorship. It may instead refer to the creator of the web site, not the generator of the information.
  - Does the web site provide information about the author(s) and their intent?

- *Purpose.* The author should be clear about the purpose of the information presented on the site. A web site may be intended to inform, persuade, state an opinion, entertain, or make fun of someone or something. The Internet often functions as a virtual "soapbox" for people or groups whose goals or aims are not clearly stated. Watch out for deliberate frauds and hoaxes.

  - What is the purpose of the page?
  - Does the domain name of the site (for example, .edu) indicate its purpose?
  - Is the information presented as fact or opinion?
  - Is evidence provided?
  - Are conclusions logical?
  - Is the information free from bias?

- Is the site free of advertising that influences that reader's view of the content?
- Is the site free of attempts to persuade or sell something?
- Is the information consistent with other material you have read on this subject? Always try to verify information you use through another source.

- *Coverage.* Web coverage of a topic is often shallow.

  - Does the web site clearly describe the topics covered?
  - Is the topic covered in depth? Or does the site cover only a specific aspect or time period for a topic?
  - Does the information add new or unique information about the topic?
  - Are there visual aids to enhance the text?
  - Does the site provide its own information instead of depending on outside links?
  - Does the site have outside links to extend the information?

- *Currency.* For scientific and technical work, information must be up-to-date. Dates are not always included on web sites or pages, and if they are they may have various meanings:

  - date first created
  - date placed on the web
  - date last revised.

Try to assess the stability of the pages you reference. One of the best ways to do this is to look closely at the site sponsor, the date of the last update, and the authority of the person or organization who provided content for the site.

  - Does the site contain either the date on the site was created or the date of the last revision?
  - Are the links to other sites live?
  - Is the information provided more up-to-date than that in a print source? Ask yourself whether or not the currency is important for the kind of information you seek.
  - Is the site complete or are there indications that the site is still under construction?

When you are writing a report and using web pages as sources, keep a backup of what you find (either as a printout or saved to disk) so that you can verify your sources later on if need be.

In addition to being central in the research process, ethical issues are increasingly important in the actual writing of the text, including the use of gendered language, descriptions of religious differences, descriptions of cultural differences, and references to sexual orientation.

Plagiarism and Copyright

Plagiarism is the theft of the work of others, either knowingly or unknowingly, by improper or inadequate documentation.

In the workplace, internal documents are treated casually, since most of the information contained in them belongs to the company. However, companies treat external documents such as technical manuals more seriously. Such documents are protected by copyright law. Use of external material requires crediting the owners of the copyright—either the company or the authors named on the document. Penalties in the workplace for copyright infringement can include lawsuits and loss of employment.

At most North American colleges and universities, plagiarism is a breach of academic integrity. Handing in a report with your name on it implies that its contents are your original work, unless otherwise indicated by the documentation system. Colleges set out penalties for inappropriate conduct in academic regulations and other campus documents.

To avoid plagiarism, write a citation for each text passage or graphic illustration from a published source, identifying the source of information for your reader. The appearance of citations in your text separates clearly your own data and ideas from the work of others.

Citations are short and give only a small part of the information that your reader needs to locate the published works that you have used in your report. Their purpose, then, is to point to a published source in your reference list. The reference list gives complete available information for each published source that you use. In this way, the citations and the reference list work together to help the reader identify a source of information without getting in the way of reading and understanding the report.

5.2 CHOOSING YOUR SYSTEM

Most scientific and technical writers document their sources with one of three widely used systems: those recommended by the Council of Science Editors (CSE), the American Psychological Association (APA), and the Modern Language Association (MLA). Each of these organizations publishes a detailed guide to its system, with descriptions of its style of citing and referencing sources and with exhaustive lists of examples.

In general, use CSE in the pure and applied sciences, APA in the social sciences, and MLA in the humanities. An alternative system, widely used in the humanities, is that outlined in *The Chicago Manual of Style*.

If you are a college student, refer to the system required in courses at your college. Consult your professors for help with CSE, APA, or MLA documentation; they know which documentation style you need to use in their courses. If you are in the workplace, consult other reports produced by professionals in the same department, company, or government agency to determine the accepted style of documentation.

Questions often arise about the details of how to cite or reference specific kinds of published information. Fortunately, answers for documentation questions are readily available. The CSE, the APA, and the MLA all publish comprehensive guides to their systems of documentation. These show examples of citations and reference entries for most types of formally and informally published material used by writers.

Internet search engines regularly list pages from North American college and university web sites that explain the popular documentation systems and give detailed examples of references and citations. Try the following:

- The New Guide to Writing Research Papers at Monroe Community College
- The OWL (Online Writing Lab) at Purdue University
- The Writing Center at the University of Wisconsin–Madison
- The Online Handbook from the Engineering Communication Program at the University of Toronto.

Scientific journals such as the *Journal of Soil and Water Conservation* and the *Journal of Wildlife Management* often use variations on the major systems. Consult these specific sources if you are submitting scientific or technical articles to a journal for publication.

5.3 THE IMPORTANCE OF CITING AND LISTING SOURCES

You must cite your sources in the text of your report at the time—and every time—you use them. You must also list complete information about each of your sources at the end of the report text. This list is a separate element. Call it "References," "List of References," "Bibliography," "Literature Cited," or "Works Cited," depending on the system of documentation you are using. Determine the correct term for the reference list in your documentation system before creating the references page in your report.

Your citations and reference list go together to give your reader complete information about which parts of your report came from secondary sources and how to find those sources. Your citation follows a graphic or a text passage showing the secondary source of information, and it points to an entry in your reference list that gives complete information about the source so that your reader can look it up.

Cite your sources thoroughly. Partial citing of sources is a common failing in student reports. Place a citation in your report at the time and every time you use source information. Cite the sources of information you used to write your text and cite the sources of tables and figures that illustrate your text.

Frequent citations are both necessary and desirable in scientific and technical reporting. Students often hesitate to place several citations on a report page. Yet this is exactly what the report writer is supposed to do: read good secondary sources and give the information to the reader. Citations show the reader that you have understood more than how to carry out your own field and lab procedures. In fact, many college report assignments require students specifically to summarize available scientific and technical literature on specific topics.

Extensive secondary research can be essential to good design of research before you begin work. Published scientific literature that describes work similar to yours will help you interpret your own results. It must appear in the literature review section of a research report.

Summarizing current information from published sources in your report also accomplishes other specific purposes. It provides the following:

- a general background of research similar to your own field or lab studies presented in the report
- a model or method for your own field or lab research presented in the report
- an authority for analysis or conclusions in your report
- a more complete explanation or set of data on your report topic.

Using Citations

Place a citation at the end of each borrowed section in your report. Borrowed sections are paraphrased summaries of the original source material. Borrowed sections vary in length; they can be a sentence, a paragraph, or a short section of two or three paragraphs under a heading. Include the citation at the end of each completed section of text before you begin a new section.

Borrowed sections of a report may combine two or more sources into a paraphrased passage. In this case, add two or more citations after the text passage. On the other hand, borrowed sections may combine two or more different passages from the same source, such as a textbook. In this case, add two or more citations that include the different page numbers for these source passages.

You may refer to the author of your source directly in your text, as in the following example: "Schneider (2004) showed isolation to be an effective method of vibration control." This technique effectively makes your reader aware of your sources of information. The author becomes part of the sentence, fully integrated with the report.

5.4 COUNCIL OF SCIENCE EDITORS (CSE)

Before 2000, the Council of Science Editors was known as the Council of Biology Editors, so you may find older references to the CBE style of documentation. The seventh edition of *The CSE Manual for Authors, Editors, and Publishers*, published in June 2006, describes two systems of documentation: the name-year system and the citation-sequence system.

The name-year system links the name of the author with the year of publication. The name-year reference list arranges your sources alphabetically by author surname.

The citation-sequence system uses simple numerals in sequence as citations in the text of your report. The citation-sequence reference list arranges your sources numerically in the order you first cite them in your text.

CSE Name-Year System

CSE Name-Year Citations

CSE name-year citations place the name of the author with the year of publication together in parentheses, or round brackets, like this: (Smith, 2004).

Forms for CSE Name-Year Citations

- *One Author.* Separate author and date with a comma: (Smith, 2004).
- *Two Authors.* Put them both in the citation: (Smith and Jones, 2004).
- *Three or More Authors.* Write only the first name followed by the abbreviation *et al,* which is Latin for "and the others": (Smith et al, 2004). Do not use *et al* in your reference list entries.
- *Source with More Than 10 Pages.* Include a page reference in the citation after a colon: (Smith et al, 2004: 245).

CSE Name-Year Reference List

Place the CSE name-year reference list on a separate page at the end of your report. It will be the last numbered page. Give it the title "References" or "References Cited." Use bold capital letters for the heading, centred at the top of the page.

Include only sources of information that you have cited, that is, written citations for sources you have cited in the text of your report. On the next page is an example of a CSE name-year reference list.

Forms for CSE Name-Year Reference Lists

Format your reference entries using single spacing and hanging indentation, which indents the second and successive lines of the entry. See Appendix D for a tutorial showing how to format a reference list using Microsoft Word XP™.

11

The most important monument at Copán is Altar Q. This limestone slab carries glyphs on all four sides and on the top. It provides us with some details about the earliest events in the reign of the first king, Kinich Yax Kuk Mo, as well as the dynastic succession of all the rulers of Copán. In one inscription, Kinich Yax Kuk Mo is said to celebrate the great, period-ending date in the Mayan calendar, 9.0.0.0.0, or December 11, 435 A.D. In all, Altar Q carries information concerning sixteen rulers of the city. The last date at Copán is associated with the last ruler, Yax Pasah. This is July 24th, 805 A.D., after which the record is silent (Coe, 1975: 142; Stuart, 2002).

Box 5.1: CSE Name-Year Citation

14

REFERENCES CITED

Coe MD. 1993. From huaquero to connoisseur: the early market in pre-Columbian art. In Collecting the pre-Columbian past. EH Boone, editor. Washington, DC: Dunbarton Oaks. pp. 271–90.

GB Online. 2002. Maya codices. GB Online's Mesoamerica. [Online]. <http://pages.prodigy.com/GBonline/mesowelc.html>. Accessed 2004 Mar 20.

Hammond N. 1982. The Maya. New Jersey: Rutgers Univ Press. 297 p.

Box 5.2: CSE Name-Year Reference List

Arrange entries in an author-date reference list alphabetically by author surname. Give the correct information in the correct order for each of your sources, following the conventions for reference entries shown below. Arrange items within entries in descending order of importance, beginning with the author, date, and title. Note that the punctuation of items within the entry is mostly periods. Separate units within the item with commas and use a colon in two cases: to introduce the second part of a two-part title and to separate the place of publication from the name of the publisher.

Examples of CSE Name-Year Reference Entries
The following examples show how to arrange CSE name-year reference list entries for commonly used types of sources.

- *Single Author*

    Erjavec J. 2000. Automotive technology: a systems approach. 3rd ed. New York: Delmar Thomson Learning. 1343 p.

- *Two Authors*

    McNair HM, Miller JM. 1997. Basic gas chromatography: techniques in analytical chemistry. New York: Wiley-Interscience. 224 p.

- *Multiple Authors*

    Griffiths AJF, Miller JH, Suzuki DT, Lewontin RC, Gelbart WM. 1996. An introduction to genetic analysis. 6th ed. New York: W.H. Freeman. 916 p.

- *Two Publications by the Same Author*

    List entries in chronological order by date of publication, with the earliest first.

    Snyder JP. 1987. Map projections: a working manual. U.S. Geological Survey Professional Paper 1395. Washington, DC: USGPO. 383 p.

    Snyder JP. 1993. Flattening the earth: two thousand years of map projections. Chicago, IL: University of Chicago Press. 365 p.

- *Two Publications by the Same Author in the Same Year*

List entries in alphabetical order by publication title. Then assign lowercase letters to each date of publication in order (2002a, 2002b, etc.).

Long JR. 2000a. A 5.1-5.8 GHz low-power image-reject downconverter. IEEE Journal of Solid-State Circuits 35: 1320–1328.

Long JR. 2000b. Monolithic transformers for silicon RF IC design. IEEE Journal of Solid-State Circuits 35: 1368–1382.

- *Book with Editor(s)*

Dorfman M, Thayer RH, editors. 1996. Software engineering. Toronto: John Wiley & Sons. 546 p.

- *Book Published in New Edition*

Diamond WJ. 2001. Practical experiment designs for engineers and scientists. 3rd ed. Toronto: John Wiley & Sons. 423 p.

- *Book Published in Volumes*

Verschueren, K. 2001. Handbook of environmental data on organic chemicals. 4th ed. 2 volumes. Weimar, TX: Culinary and Hospitality Industry Publications Services. 2391 p.

- *Article in an Encyclopedia*

Hinrichs T. 1992. Geothermal power. McGraw-Hill encyclopedia of science and technology. 7th ed. New York: McGraw-Hill 8: 83–87.

- *Article in a Scholarly Journal*

Brett NC. 1991. Language laws and collective rights. The Canadian Journal of Law and Jurisprudence 4(2): 347–360.

- *Article in a Monthly Periodical*

Ricciardelli A, Pizzimenti D, Mattei M. 2003. Passive and active mass damper control of the response of tall buildings to wind gustiness. Engineering Structures 25(9): 1199–1209.

- *Article in a Newspaper*

  Palmer K. 2003 May 7. West Nile plan outlined: province vows to increase spending. Toronto Star; Sect B: 5.

- *Article without an Author*

  [Anonymous]. 2003 July 11. Biotech crops get third-world boost. The Globe and Mail; Sect C: 4.

- *Video Recording*

  Decision making and problem solving. 1990. [videocassette]. Coast Community College District; Toronto: TVOntario; 1990. 28 min, sound, colour, ½ in.

- *Article in an Online Journal*

  Wang, F, Juniper SK, Pelegrí SP, Macko SA. 2003. Denitrification in sediments of the Laurentian Trough, St. Lawrence Estuary, Québec, Canada. Estuarine, Coastal and Shelf Science. [serial online]. 57(3):515-522. Available from: http://www.sciencedirect.com/science/journal/02727714. Accessed 2003 Jul 16.

- *Article on a CD-ROM*

  Nichols M. 1995. High-tech artificial limbs. Maclean's. 13 March 1995. The Canadian encyclopedia 2001 [CD-ROM]. Toronto: McClelland & Stewart, 2000.

- *E-mail*

  Birnstihl J. Re: Update. [personal e-mail]. info@cdta.bidcon.net. Accessed 2006 May 12.

- *Web Page*

  Maddison DR, Maddison WP, Schulz KS, Wheeler T, Frumkin J. 2001. The Tree of Life Web Project. [online]. Available from: http://tolweb.org. Accessed 2006 Jul 15.

- *Article from a Subscription Service or Online Database*

  Bergman, B. 2003 June 23. Born to be high and wild. Maclean's 116(25). EBSCOhost Academic Search Premier. Rogers Media, Publishing Ltd. Item 10046413. Accessed 2006 Sep 30.

CSE Citation-Sequence System

CSE Citation-Sequence Citations

Citations in the CSE citation-sequence system are labelled using simple Arabic numerals placed in parentheses, such as the following: (1).

As with name-year citations, place citation numerals at the end of each borrowed section in your report. Borrowed sections may combine two or more sources into a paraphrased passage, with two or more citation-sequence numerals appearing after the text passage.

Assign a numeral to each of your sources in the order that you first use and cite its information in your report. For example, if Smith is the source for the first section of your text, give it the numeral "1." This number then identifies Smith in your reference list. If Jones is the next source you have used in your report, assign it the numeral "2," and so on.

Notice that each source has only one citation numeral. If you decide to use material from Smith later in your report, cite Smith with the numeral "1" again. Do not assign Smith another numeral.

CSE Citation-Sequence Reference List

Place the CSE citation-sequence reference list on a separate page at the end of your report. It will be the last numbered page. Give it the title "References" or "References Cited." Use bold capital letters for the heading centred at the top of the page.

Include only those sources of information that you have cited, that is, written citations for, in the text of your report.

Format your reference entries using single spacing. Use the hanging indentation format for a numbered list. The second and successive lines of each entry should begin directly below the first letter of the first word on the first line of the entry.

Arrange your reference entries in numerical order according to the numbers that you have assigned to your sources in the report text.

Examples of CSE Citation-Sequence Reference Entries

The order of items within each citation-sequence entry is the same as in each name-year entry; only the order of entries in the list is different. List the citation-sequence sources in numerical order. Each has a number that you assigned to the source when you first paraphrased its information in your report.

10

The most important monument at Copán is Altar Q. This limestone slab carries glyphs on all four sides and on the top. It provides us with some details about the earliest events in the reign of the first king, Kinich Yax Kuk Mo, as well as the dynastic succession of all the rulers of Copán. In one inscription, Kinich Yax Kuk Mo is said to celebrate the great, period-ending date in the Mayan calendar, 9.0.0.0.0, or December 11, 435 A.D. In all, Altar Q carries information concerning sixteen rulers of the city. The last date at Copán is associated with the last ruler, Yax Pasah. This is July 24th, 805 A.D., after which the record is silent (2, 3).

Box 5.3: CSE Citation-Sequence Citation

The format for the citation-sequence list entries is the indented block with the number of the entry on the left margin of the page, as shown in the sample citation-sequence reference list.

14

REFERENCES

1. GB Online. 2002. Maya codices. GB Online's Mesoamerica. [Online]. Available from: http://pages.prodigy.com/GBonline/ mesowelc.html. Accessed 2004 Mar 20.

2. Coe MD. 1993. From huaquero to connoisseur: the early market in pre-Columbian art. In Collecting the pre-Columbian past. EH Boone, ed. Washington, DC: Dunbarton Oaks. pp. 271–90.

3. Hammond N. 1982. The Maya. New Jersey: Rutgers University Press.

Box 5.4: CSE Citation-Sequence Reference List

5.5 AMERICAN PSYCHOLOGICAL ASSOCIATION (APA)

The APA system has been in use since 1929. The fifth edition of the APA *Publication Manual* appeared in 2001. In the APA style, citations consist of the author's surname and the date of publication in parentheses, that is, round brackets. Complete information about each source is listed alphabetically by author surname at the end of the report in the reference list.

APA Author-Date Citations

To make an APA citation for a paraphrased section in your report, place the name of the author followed by a comma and the year of publication together in parentheses, or round brackets, like this: (Smith, 2004). If you quote from your source directly in your report, add the page number to your citation, like this: (Smith, 2004, p. 105). Introduce an APA author-date citation in the text with a phrase that includes the author's surname, followed by the date in parentheses; for example, "When similar metal fibres were tested by Johnson and Hubbard (2002), tensile strengths of 600 to 800 g were recorded."

Forms for APA Author-Date Citations

- *One Author.* Include the author's surname, followed by a comma and a date: (Smith, 2004)
- *Two Authors.* Use an ampersand to connect the authors' surnames: (Johnson & Hubbard, 2002).
- *No Author.* Cite the source by using the first two or three significant words of the title: ("Biotech crops," 2003).
- *Three or More Authors.* List all authors the first time you cite their work: (James, Harrison, Wilson, McAlpine, & Fingaard, 2003). The second and successive times you cite their work, list only the first name followed by "et al": (James et al, 2003).

10

The most important monument at Copán is Altar Q (Coe, 1975). This limestone slab carries glyphs on all four sides and on the top. It provides us with some details about the earliest events in the reign of the first king, Kinich Yax Kuk Mo, as well as the dynastic succession of all the rulers of Copán. In one inscription, Kinich Yax Kuk Mo is said to celebrate the great, period-ending date in the Mayan calendar, 9.0.0.0.0, or December 11, 435 A.D. In all, Altar Q carries information concerning sixteen rulers of the city. As epigrapher David Stuart (2002, p. 16) has concluded, "The last date at Copán is associated with the last ruler, Yax Pasah. This is July 24th, 805 A.D., after which the record is silent."

Box 5.5: APA Citation

- *Corporate Author.* Write out the name of the organization the first time you cite their work and include the abbreviation of that organization in square brackets: (The American Radio Relay League [ARRL], 1997). Use the abbreviation in second and successive citations: (ARRL, 1997).
- *E-mail.* Note that APA documentation does not include personal communications in the reference list. In the text, cite it with the name of the sender, an identifying phrase, and the date: (J. Birnstihl, personal communication, May 12, 2003).

APA Author-Date Reference List

List all sources you cited in the text of your report under the centred heading "References."

It is acceptable in APA style to use either hanging indentation or regular indented paragraph format for entries in reference lists. Whichever format you choose, use it consistently throughout the list. Double-space your entries.

List your sources in alphabetical order by author's surname. If you have more than one source by the same author, list the sources by date of publication, oldest first. If you have more than one source by the same author in the same year, list the sources in alphabetical order by title and add lowercase letters to the dates of publication, like this: (Smith, 2003a) (Smith, 2003b).

Titles of separate works such as books and journals are placed in italics or underlined. The dates of publication following the author's name are placed in parentheses.

Examples of APA Author-Date Reference Entries

- *Single Author*

  Erjavec, J. (2000). *Automotive technology: A systems approach* (3rd ed.). Clifton Park, NY: Thomson Delmar Learning.

- *Two Authors*

  McNair, H. M., & Miller, J. M. (1997). *Basic gas chromatography: Techniques in analytical chemistry*. New York: Wiley-Interscience.

14

REFERENCES

Coe, M. D. (1993). From huaquero to connoisseur: The early market in
pre-Columbian art. In E.H. Boone (Ed.)., *Collecting the pre-
Columbian past* (pp. 271–90). Washington, D.C.: Dunbarton
Oaks.

GB Online. (2002). Maya codices. GB Online's Mesoamerica. Retrieved
March 20, 2004, from http://pages.prodigy.com/GBonline/
mesowelc.html

Hammond, N. (1982). *The Maya*. New Jersey: Rutgers University Press.

Box 5.6: APA Author-Date Reference List

- *Multiple Authors*

  Griffiths, A. J. F., J. H. Miller, D. T. Suzuki, R. C. Lewontin, & W. M. Gelbart. (1996). *An introduction to genetic analysis* (6th ed.). New York: W. H. Freeman.

- *Two Publications by the Same Author*

  List entries in chronological order by date of publication, earliest first.

  Snyder, J. P. (1987). *Map projections: A working manual.* U.S. Geological Survey Professional Paper 1395. Washington, DC: USGPO.

  Snyder, J. P. (1993). *Flattening the earth: Two thousand years of map projections.* Chicago, IL: University of Chicago Press.

- *Two Publications by the Same Author in the Same Year*

  Long, J. R. (2000a). A 5.1–5.8 GHz low-power image-reject downconverter. *IEEE Journal of Solid-State Circuits, 35,* 1320–1328.

  Long, J. R. (2000b). Monolithic transformers for silicon RF IC design. *IEEE Journal of Solid-State Circuits, 35,* 1368–1382.

- *Book with Editor(s)*

  Dorfman, M, & R. H. Thayer. (Eds.). (1996). *Software engineering.* Toronto: John Wiley & Sons.

- *Book Published in a New Edition*

  Diamond, W. J. (2001). *Practical experiment designs for engineers and scientists* (3rd ed.). Toronto: John Wiley & Sons.

- *Book Published in Volumes*

  Verschueren, K. (2001). *Handbook of environmental data on organic chemicals* (4th ed., Vols. 1–2). Weimar, TX: Culinary and Hospitality Industry Publications Services.

- *Article in an Encyclopedia*

  Hinrichs, T. (1992). Geothermal power. In *McGraw-Hill encyclopedia of science and technology* (7th ed., Vol. 8, pp. 83–87). New York: McGraw-Hill.

- *Article in a Scholarly Journal*

  Brett, N. C. (1991). Language laws and collective rights. *The Canadian Journal of Law and Jurisprudence 4*(2), 347–360.

- *Article in a Monthly Periodical*

  Ricciardelli, A., D. Pizzimenti, & M. Mattei. (2003). Passive and active mass damper control of the response of tall buildings to wind gustiness. *Engineering Structures 25*(9), 1199–1209.

- *Article in a Newspaper*

  Palmer, K. (2003, May 7). West Nile plan outlined: Province vows to increase spending. *Toronto Star*, p. B5.

- *Article without an Author*

  List the article alphabetically by title.

  Biotech crops get third-world boost. (2003, July 11). *The Globe and Mail*, p. C4.

- *Video Recording*

  List alphabetically by director or producer. This form of entry can also be used for audiotape, slides, and film.

  Coast Community College District (Producer). (1990). *Decision making and problem solving.* [Videocassette]. Toronto: TVOntario.

- *Article in an Online Journal*

  Wang, F., S. K. Juniper, S. P. Pelegrí, & S. A. Macko. (2003). Denitrification in sediments of the Laurentian Trough, St. Lawrence Estuary, Québec, Canada. *Estuarine, Coastal and Shelf Science, 57*(3), 515–522. Retrieved July 16, 2003, from http://www.sciencedirect.com/science/journal/02727714

• *Article on a CD-ROM*

Nichols, M. (1995, March 13). High-tech artificial limbs. *Maclean's*. Retrieved October 23, 2006, from *The Canadian Encyclopedia 2001*. [CD-ROM]. Toronto: McClelland & Stewart.

• *E-mail*

Do not include personal communications in an APA reference list.

• *Web Page*

Maddison, D. R., W. P. Maddison, K. S. Schulz, T. Wheeler, & J. Frumkin. (2001). *The Tree of Life Web Project*. [Online]. Retrieved July 15, 2006, from http://tolweb.org

• *Article from a Subscription Service or Online Database*

Bergman, B. (2003, June 23). Born to be high and wild. *Maclean's*, *116*(25). Retrieved September 30, 2006, from *EBSCOhost Academic Search Premier*. Rogers Media Publishing Ltd. Item 10046413.

5.6 MODERN LANGUAGE ASSOCIATION (MLA)

The Modern Language Association has been publishing style guidelines for scholars in modern languages since 1951. The MLA style of documentation has recently preferred parenthetical citations and works cited over footnotes and bibliography. The sixth edition of the *MLA Handbook for Writers of Research Papers* for high school and undergraduate college students was published in 2003. The second edition of the *MLA Style Manual and Guide to Scholarly Publishing* for graduate students, scholars, and professional writers was published in 1998.

MLA Parenthetical Citations

An MLA parenthetical citation consists of the first word used to identify the source in the list of works cited, usually the author's surname, and the page number where the information for the report was found, if one is available. It looks like this: (Smith 328). Note that each citation is enclosed in round brackets and contains no punctuation.

10

The most important monument at Copán is Altar Q (Coe 174). This limestone slab carries glyphs on all four sides and on the top. It provides us
with some details about the earliest events in the reign of the first king,
Kinich Yax Kuk Mo, as well as the dynastic succession of all the rulers
of Copán. In one inscription, Kinich Yax Kuk Mo is said to celebrate the
great, period-ending date in the Mayan calendar, 9.0.0.0.0, or December
11, 435 A.D. In all, Altar Q carries information concerning sixteen rulers
of the city. As epigrapher David Stuart (16) has concluded, "The last
date at Copán is associated with the last ruler, Yax Pasah. This is July
24th, 805 A.D., after which the record is silent."

Box 5.7: MLA Parenthetical Citations

Forms for MLA Parenthetical Citations

- *One Author.* Provide author surname and the number of the page on which you found the information you used: (Smith 328).
- *Two Authors.* Put them both in the citation: (Smith and Jones 328).
- *Three or More Authors.* Write all authors' names or use the first name only: (Smith, Jones, and Tremblay 328) or (Smith 328).
- *Book Published in Several Volumes.* Include the volume number in the citation: (Smith, v.2: 328).
- *Corporate Author.* (Texas Instruments 16)
- *No Author.* Cite by the first word of the title, remembering that titles of books are italicized while titles of articles are placed in quotation marks: ("Joint" 194).

MLA Works Cited List

List all sources you cited in the text of your report alphabetically by author surname under the centred heading Works Cited (see Box 5.8). Set up the entries with hanging indentation and double spacing. Sometimes you will read published sources that prepare you to write your paper but that you do not incorporate into your report in any way. These are uncited sources. Some report readers may wish to dig deeper into the subject of your report beyond the list of cited sources. Therefore, you may add a list of uncited sources after the Works Cited list; for this second list, use the title Works Consulted. Use the same format as in the "Works Cited" list.

If you have more than one source by the same author, list the sources alphabetically by title. For the second entry, use three hyphens in place of the author's name. To cite these in your text, use the author's name and keywords from the title to distinguish the different sources; for example, (Smith *Amanuensis* 36), (Smith *Blathering* 599).

Place the titles of independent works, such as books and journals, in italic typeface or underline them. Capitalize each significant word in the title. Place the date of publication following the publication information.

For an authored chapter in an edited book, list the author and title of the chapter first. Then list the title, editor, and other details of the book.

Enclose Universal Resource Locators (URLs) for web pages with angle brackets: < and >.

14

WORKS CITED

Coe, Michael D. "From Huaquero to Connoisseur: The Early Market in

    Pre-Columbian Art." *Collecting the Pre-Columbian Past.* Ed. E.H.

    Boone. Washington, DC: Dunbarton Oaks, 1993. 271–90.

GB Online. "Maya codices." *GB Online's Mesoamerica.* 2002. 20 Mar.

    2004 <http: //pages.prodigy.com/GBonline/mesowelc.html>.

Hammond, Norman. *The Maya.* New Jersey: Rutgers UP, 1982.

Box 5.8: MLA Works Cited List

Examples of MLA Works Cited Reference Entries

- *Single Author*

    Erjavec, Jack. *Automotive Technology: A Systems Approach.* 3rd ed. Clifton Park,
        NY: Thomson Delmar Learning, 2000.

- *Two Authors*

    McNair, Harold M., and James M. Miller. *Basic Gas Chromatography: Techniques
        in Analytical Chemistry.* New York: Wiley-Interscience, 1997.

- *Multiple Authors*

    Griffiths, Anthony J.F., Jeffery H. Miller, David T. Suzuki, Richard C. Lewontin,
        and William M. Gelbart. *An Introduction to Genetic Analysis.* 6th ed. New
        York: W.H. Freeman, 1996.

- *Two Publications by the Same Author*

    List entries in alphabetical order by title. Insert three hyphens in
    place of the author's name in the second listing to show that it is the
    work of the same author as above.

    Snyder, John P. *Map Projections: A Working Manual.* U.S. Geological Survey
        Professional Paper 1395. Washington, DC: USGPO, 1987.

    ---. *Flattening the Earth: Two Thousand Years of Map Projections.* Chicago, IL:
        University of Chicago Press, 1993.

- *Book with Editor(s)*

    Dorfman, Merlin, and Richard H. Thayer, eds. *Software Engineering.* Toronto:
        John Wiley & Sons, 1996.

- *Book Published in New Edition*

    Diamond, William J. *Practical Experiment Designs for Engineers and Scientists.*
        3rd ed. Toronto: John Wiley & Sons, 2001.

- *Book Published in Volumes*

Verschueren, Karen. *Handbook of Environmental Data on Organic Chemicals.* 4th ed. 2 vols. Weimar, TX: Culinary and Hospitality Industry Publications Services, 2001.

- *Article in an Encyclopedia*

Hinrichs, Thomas. "Geothermal Power." *McGraw-Hill Encyclopedia of Science and Technology.* 7th ed. (Vol. 8, pp. 83–87). New York: McGraw-Hill, 1992.

- *Article in a Scholarly Journal*

Brett, Nathan C. "Language Laws and Collective Rights." *The Canadian Journal of Law and Jurisprudence* 4.2 (1991): 347–60.

- *Article in a Monthly Periodical*

Ricciardelli, A., D. Pizzimenti, and M. Mattei. "Passive and Active Mass Damper Control of the Response of Tall Buildings to Wind Gustiness." *Engineering Structures* 25.9 (2003): 1199–1209.

- *Article in a Newspaper*

Palmer, Karen. "West Nile Plan Outlined: Province Vows to Increase Spending." *Toronto Star* 7 May 2003: B5.

- *Article without an Author*

List the article alphabetically by title.

"Biotech Crops Get Third-World Boost." *The Globe and Mail* 11 July 2003: C4.

- *Video Recording*

List alphabetically by title.

Decision Making and Problem Solving. Videocassette. Coast Community College District. Toronto: TVOntario. 1990.

- *Article in an Online Journal*

    Wang, Fenghai, S. Kim Juniper, Silvia P. Pelegrí, and Stephen A. Macko. "Denitrification in Sediments of the Laurentian Trough, St. Lawrence Estuary, Québec, Canada." *Estuarine, Coastal and Shelf Science* 57.3 (2003): 515–22. 16 July 2003 <http://www.sciencedirect.com/science/journal/02727714>.

- *Article on a CD-ROM*

    Nichols, Mark. "High-Tech Artificial Limbs." *Maclean's* 13 March 1995. *The Canadian Encyclopedia 2001.* CD-ROM. Toronto: McClelland & Stewart, 2000.

- *E-mail*

    Birnstihl, Jennifer. "Re: Update." E-mail to Professor C.L. Gulston. 12 May 2006.

- *Web Page*

    Maddison, David R., Wayne P. Maddison, Katja S. Schulz, Travis Wheeler, and Jeremy Frumkin. The Tree of Life Web Project. 15 Jul 2006 <http://tolweb.org>.

- *Article from a Subscription Service or Online Database*

    Bergman, Brian. "Born to Be High and Wild." *Maclean's* 23 June 2003. Retrieved 30 September 2006, from *EBSCOhost Academic Search Premier.* Rogers Media Publishing Ltd. Item 10046413. Sir Sandford Fleming College LRC <http://fleming0.flemingc.on.ca/lrc/library/libav2.htm>.

CHECKLIST FOR REPORT DOCUMENTATION

During your research, be sure that you have done the following:

- Chosen the correct system of documentation: CSE, APA, MLA, or other.
- Cited and listed in references all sources used in the report.

When using a system of documentation, be sure that you have done the following:

CSE Name-Year System

- Placed a citation after each borrowed text passage and graphic presentation in the report.
- Placed citations in parentheses, with author surname and year of publication: (Smith, 2004).
- Called the reference list References or References Cited.
- Organized the References Cited list in alphabetical order by author surname.
- Used hanging indentation format, single-spaced.
- Ensured that all entries have complete information and correct order of items.

CSE Citation-Sequence System

- Placed a citation after each borrowed text passage and graphic presentation in the report.
- Used Arabic numerals for citations, in parentheses: (1), (2), etc.
- Called the reference list References or References Cited.
- Organized the References Cited list in numerical order, single-spaced.
- Ensured that all entries have complete information and correct order of items.

APA

- Placed a citation after each borrowed text passage and graphic presentation in the report.
- Put citations in parentheses, with author surname and publication year: (Smith, 2004).
- For direct quotations, included page number: (Smith, 2004, p. 105).
- Called the reference list References.
- Listed sources in alphabetical order.
- Double-spaced reference entries and used either regular indentation or handing indent format.
- Ensured that all entries have complete information and correct order of items.

MLA

- Placed a citation after each borrowed text passage and graphic presentation in the report.
- Put citations in parentheses, including author's name or first word from Works Cited list and page number.
- Called the reference list Works Cited.
- Checked to see whether additional Works Consulted list is required.
- Listed sources in alphabetical order.
- Double-spaced reference entries and used either regular indentation or handing indent format.
- Ensured that whole publication titles are in italics or underlined and partial publication titles are enclosed in quotation marks.
- Ensured that all entries have complete information and correct order of items.

C h a p t e r

Presentation Skills

6

Overview: This chapter sets out a method for developing and delivering an effective oral presentation of technical information. It also describes a way of effectively using multimedia to support an oral presentation.

6.1 ORAL PRESENTATIONS

The Value of Presentations

Presentation skills and writing skills are partners in the dance of professional communications. Writing leads and presenting follows. Writing lets you pull all your information together, organize it, and analyze it. Presenting lets you deliver the information and insights gained from writing directly to an audience, the people in your professional community.

Good speakers are good leaders. If you can't communicate, you can't command. The most important success factor in your career is your ability to make contact with an audience, inform them, and move them to action. Presentations transmit much more information in a shorter time period than a written report can. Presenting communicates your attitudes and personality; it involves an audience in your world, interests them in your subject through your enthusiasm and energy, builds their trust in you, and persuades them of your viewpoint.

Presenting also gives you an opportunity to grow and learn, to exchange ideas and information with others in your professional community. Questions following your presentation allow an audience to pursue issues that you've raised; they give you valuable feedback about your presentation.

Public Speaking

According to the *Book of Lists* (Wallechinsky and Wallace, 1993), the greatest fear of most North American adults is public speaking. According to most career counsellors, public speaking is an essential competence, a skill mastered by all successful professionals. It seems reasonable then for people working in science, technology, and engineering to overcome this fear and develop a level of comfort and competence with audiences of varied sizes and types.

The keys to comfort in a presentation are the following three Ps:

- preparation
- practice
- prior success.

Be well prepared. Do your homework. Make sure you have looked at the big picture and selected the best, most relevant ideas and information for your audience. Choose a simple and effective organization plan for your presentation so that you will know what to do next and so that your audience will be able to fit the facts together and make sense of them as you speak.

Smooth delivery takes practice. Work with your materials. Put the organization plan together with the details of your presentation and with your audiovisual materials. Practise in front of a mirror. Practise on friends and family. Practise on small groups of people before attempting larger ones. Join Toastmasters International in your community to learn and practise your speaking skills in a relaxed, fun atmosphere.

Beyond smooth delivery is confidence. Audiences know immediately when a practised professional is speaking to them because they sense a presence, a sureness of thought and word that comes with having been successful with other audiences. When you have finished a presentation and see in people's friendly smiles and in their demeanour the impact you've had, you will know that you have given them something positive, and that knowledge will give you greater self-assurance in the next presentation. This feeling grows as you accept and work through the challenges of each new presentation. By the way, your confidence also helps the audience, who will relax, enjoy the presentation, and get more out of it.

As you have seen from previous chapters, developing data and reporting it in science and technology often requires a team approach. The same is true of presenting. Your audience will want to see and hear the whole team and, if possible, ask them questions. A team presentation requires more work to coordinate the contributions of each member, but it has great advantages. Teamwork means better preparation, so essential to good presenting. Members catch each others' mistakes and deepen each others' research. Delivering the presentation together means mutual support and less focus on you individually if you happen to be nervous. Team members can prompt you when you get stuck for the next point, put up the next slide for you, or engage in illuminating dialogue with you. Good teams make good presentations.

Extemporaneous Speech
The form of presentation most used in science and technology is called extemporaneous speech. This is a talk that is planned but not scripted. It requires that you have enough expertise and enough immediate information in your head that you can speak fluently and confidently about your subject, using only an outline of points to organize your talk. An extemporaneous speech is created as you speak out of your knowledge base, and it requires an ability to choose and deliver appropriate ideas and information to your audience on the spot.

Audience and Purpose
Knowing your audience and purpose is as important to a presentation as it is to a report. It affects every choice you make about content and style of presentation. Take time before selecting and organizing materials for your presentation to think about your audience and their needs. If possible, contact someone connected to the presentation and ask specific questions about the audience's specific interests and expectations, including time limits. Here are some of the audiences to whom you can expect to speak:

- *Clients and customers.* Technical sales and service is an important area of employment, including self-employment, for graduates in science, technical, and engineering professions. Consultants in all professional fields must expect to speak to clients about their work.

- *People in your organization.* Co-workers need information updates or leadership on committees. Managers need reporting on current activities and assessment of results.
- *Professionals in your field.* Conference presentations are important for your career development and for your company.
- *Public audiences.* Professionals can expect to speak to public audiences in different situations, from giving group tours around the plant to delivering outdoor education to increasing public awareness of law enforcement.

Consider your audience's key characteristics. What level of expertise do they have? How uniform is your audience in age or professional experience or cultural background? What are their expectations for your talk in terms of length, content, and style of presentation? Answers to these and other questions will tell you what needs to be included in the presentation and how to develop it.

The most common purpose for speaking in science and technology is information. Professional audiences are thirsty for specific details on a wide variety of subjects. In fact, presenters sometimes underestimate how much information a professional audience of scientists, technicians, or engineers needs. Other, more general audiences, require a careful selection of technical information because they can be easily overwhelmed with details.

As you progress in your career, you will need to present information in such a way as to persuade the audience to do something that you feel is important. Presentations that persuade are indispensable in your career, and they require a careful analysis of your audience: their needs, concerns, and motivations. A presentation that solves the audience's problems and answers their concerns will motivate them to action: writing a contract, setting up an employee wellness program, or using more efficient enforcement methods. The list is endless.

Preparing Presentations

Find your facts. Good research is essential to a presentation on a scientific or technical subject because the audience expects expertise—a depth of knowledge and insight in your special field. At the same time, you will feel more comfortable and relaxed in front of an audience because you feel confident of your subject.

Make an outline—that is, a logical sequence of main points and subpoints. Most audiences will tell you that the worst mistake a presenter can make is to wander from one topic to another without connections or sense of organization. Keep your plan simple; this allows an audience to stay oriented as they listen to the details. Organize the details into four main points maximum. Remember that you will add an introduction and concluding remarks. Arrange the details under each main topic with the most important points first and give the first points more attention.

Add your introduction and concluding remarks. Then decide on the supporting materials you will need: props, slides, multimedia, and so on.

Introductions

Your primary goal when introducing your presentation is to tell your audience your purpose in speaking to them, how your subject connects to their needs and concerns. Include a list of the main topics you will cover so they will have a plan to follow and be able to remember the details you present. In most cases, you will also need to fill in necessary background information: the history of a particular problem, the development of a new technology, the operating theory of instrumentation used, and so on.

You may have other goals for your introduction. If your audience is young or likely to arrive distracted by circumstances, you will need to gain their attention. This can be accomplished in a variety of ways:

- a personal anecdote, relevant example, or current incident
- a famous quotation or startling statistic
- a challenging question or idea
- a brief demonstration
- a striking visual, such as a cartoon.

With professional audiences, you may wish to establish your credibility by describing briefly your current position, your previous projects and work experience, or your educational background. When your goal is to persuade, it is important in your introduction to establish rapport with your audience by describing interests you have in common.

Supporting Materials

People have a limited time to see, hear, and understand you. The 50/50 rule of public speaking says that 50 percent of your audience pays attention 50 percent of the time. This rough rule points to an essential truth. To get your most important points across, you must first focus the attention of the audience so that most of them are listening as you speak. This is the first purpose of using good supporting materials.

It is also true that people focus on and remember specific experiences, and through them they learn general ideas and principles. Supporting materials that include specific examples and solid, relevant illustrations accomplish this goal.

Good supporting materials must be

- interesting to the audience
- relevant to your subject and purpose
- accurate so as not to mislead
- personal, in that they are somehow connected to your life and work.

Types of supporting materials that you may choose include the following:

- examples and illustrations
- statistics in graphic form to show trends or patterns
- comparisons to connect the unfamiliar with the familiar
- quotations from experts, good especially for explaining principles
- maps for spatial information to orient audience
- diagrams and flow charts for technical processes
- language signposts—that is, text visuals that preview or summarize points.

Concluding Remarks

Concluding remarks are an emphatic part of a presentation. The audience will be listening carefully. Summarize your main points and review the most important details. Choose a simple option for ending:

- immediate and future trends
- inspirational appeal
- quotation from an authority
- challenge to action.

Practice Sessions

Test drive your presentation to find the weak areas:

- material you don't know well
- questionable information—be sure to double check it
- missing pieces and transitions between main points
- time limit problems
- fit between your supporting materials and your talk.

Delivering Presentations

A few essentials to remember while speaking will keep your presentation lively, smooth, and professional.

Maintain eye contact. Move your field of vision around the entire audience. Don't focus on one or two people. Include the whole group.

Speak slowly and loudly enough to be heard at the back of the room. If you need a microphone, be sure one is available and in working order. Maintain a steady pace without long pauses. Speak with expression; slightly exaggerate your natural speaking style to emphasize important points.

Avoid annoying gestures. Be aware of gestures. Use positive ones that come naturally to you to emphasize important points in your presentation.

Ensure that visuals are large enough to be seen by the whole audience. Know your supporting materials. Know when, where, and how you want to use them to support your presentation.

Nervousness is the most common problem faced by presenters. To combat nervousness, avoid food and drink with caffeine immediately before the presentation. Take deep, relaxing breaths before speaking. Inventory your muscles; relax any muscle groups that have become tense. Find friendly, interested faces in the audience and speak to them.

In team presentations, share time equally. Listen to each other speak; the audience will notice if you appear inattentive. Decide on the division of labour for the presentation: which members will present which sections of the presentation, which will use which supporting materials, which supporting materials will require a team effort, and so on.

6.2 THE USE OF MULTIMEDIA

Multimedia has many applications in a presentation. It can

- immerse a viewer in an experience
- explain and clarify concepts and processes
- focus audience attention on key points
- sustain audience interest to the end of the presentation.

Advantages of Multimedia Software

Multimedia or presentation software is the most widely used method of supporting an oral presentation in science and technology because it has many advantages:

- Presentation software combines visual, textual, and audio elements in a single application.
- Presentation software is flexible, powerful, and relatively simple to use in creating a presentation.
- Digital presentation files are easily altered, requiring little effort to update information or refocus the presentation for a different audience.
- For conferences and workshops, digital presentation files are easy to transport on a laptop, CD, or a portable storage device (such as a USB drive or a memory stick).
- Digital presentation files can be used to create printed material or to publish on the web for a wider audience.

Presentation software is fun to use. It is a creative tool, so experiment! The capability of a multimedia software package will challenge your creativity and give you new ways to make contact with an audience. When preparing a presentation, do not be afraid of mistakes; you can always erase and start again.

The Nature of Multimedia

Multimedia software is designed to allow the average computer user to integrate and display text and graphic and/or audio information together in a series of slides which can be projected onto a screen. This capability makes it a flexible tool for supporting oral presentations in a classroom, at a sales meeting, during training sessions, or in any group presentation. An oral presentation supported with multimedia requires a computer with the multimedia application, the digital presentation files, and a data projector.

The discipline of using multimedia software lies in adapting organized, outlined content to a series of slides. Content from reports, field notes, or web research can be complex, but multimedia slides are limited in scope. Therefore, you will need a storyboard approach to each main idea you want to introduce and explain, breaking it into small increments, each of which, in turn, can be fit easily onto a single slide. Each main idea, then, becomes a sequence of simple slides containing bulleted short lists of points and simple graphics illustrating those points. Develop the habit of thinking in logically connected sequences of small, focused bits.

Working with Multimedia

The following is a simple process for developing an effective multimedia presentation. Keep in mind that multimedia can make a good presentation better and a bad presentation worse. Ensure that you already have a presentation that is well researched and organized before attempting to use multimedia.

Open a blank presentation in your multimedia software. Each of the following steps requires a complete pass through the slide sequence in the presentation. Use the process to edit slide content and check for appropriate sequencing of elements.

- Select a suitable design for your presentation. Most multimedia software comes with a set of professionally designed templates that set the slide backgrounds, colours, and typefaces for text. Unless you have experience in graphic design, use one of these templates, preferably one with a simple background that does not distract your audience from your text and graphics.
- Write the text for your slide sequence first. Text is the key to good organization in your presentation. Break each section of your presentation into a series of titled slides. Specific, descriptive slide titles will focus the audience's attention on specific topics as you speak. Write point-form notes, no more than six words on a line and no more than six lines on a slide. Use the spell check function; spelling errors projected on a large screen to your audience will cost you credibility.

- When you have completed the slide sequence using text only, lay out the media you want to illustrate the text on each slide. You may wish to add graphic-only slides to the text slides or leave some slides as text-only. Variety in layout works best. In multimedia, graphic presentations can include digital images, digital video, and digital sounds. Label your images with text boxes to identify maps, graphs, charts, and so on for your audience. Note that sound and video files cannot be incorporated into the presentation file; they require an active link, so it is best to keep all multimedia files together in the same folder on your computer.

- Add transitions and animations. Without transitions and animations, each slide will appear whole to your audience on a mouse click or keyboard command, unless you have automated a slide sequence. Professional presenters prefer not to automate so they can control the speed of slide delivery to match the pacing of their talk. Transitions make each new slide appear gradually in a variety of ways instead of flashing suddenly on the screen. Transitions signal to the audience that a new slide is appearing and refocus their attention on the content. Choose simple transitions without sound; flamboyant transitions are distracting and inappropriate for a professional audience. In addition, the text and media on individual slides can be animated if you wish them to appear separately after the slide itself has appeared. This will depend on how and when you wish to speak about the content of the slide; you may wish to introduce text and graphics for key concepts individually on a mouse click on a slide.

- Sort and test your slide sequence. The slide sorting function in your software allows you to see the whole sequence and adjust the position of individual slides in the sequence. Test drive your presentation on your computer monitor, ensuring that the slides, animations, and transitions are working as you wish. Practise how you will speak to each slide. Edit ruthlessly where necessary. Keep your slides simple.

Speaker's notes can be added to individual slides and printed to guide you through detailed presentations. Slides can also be printed in various formats to make handouts for the audience. Remember to hand out detailed materials only at the end of your presentation so as not to distract the audience from your talk. You can also publish your multimedia presentation on the Internet to reach a wider audience.

Guidelines for Presenting with Multimedia

Do not read your visuals aloud as you present; members of your audience can read for themselves. You will lose credibility if you read your own text because it will appear that you have not prepared adequately for the presentation.

Allow time for the audience to read visuals. Charts, graphics, cutaway drawings, digital photographs, and schematic diagrams carry a great deal of information. Budget enough time to describe the important features of the graphic while the audience absorbs the visual impact and processes the information. For the same reason, do not present complicated or inappropriate visuals. For example, showing a general audience in a provincial park a table of raw data asks them to interpret beyond their abilities, resulting in frustration for them.

Use occasional text-only visuals to preview or summarize sections of the presentation or to list important points. People read from top down, so place important points at the top. Use a bulleted list when all your points are equally important. When the list is prioritized or represents steps in a process, use a numbered list.

For multimedia presentations, use sounds sparingly. Audiences have a low tolerance for sounds. Keep sound bites short. Use music to set a mood at the beginning of your talk or sounds to identify specific items, such as bird calls. Video is the most powerful medium used in presentations, getting the audience closest to direct experience. However, digital video files in most formats tend to be large. Full-screen, full-motion video can be problematic within a presentation software. Audiences generally prefer to hear your expertise instead of watching a lengthy video. Keep video clips short and specific to illustrate your points.

Most importantly, apply the principles of good presenting. Design your presentation for your audience and purpose. Then design your multimedia with your speech in mind. Do not attempt to improvise during your presentation—for example, use a freehand screen pen to draw—unless you are practised at it. Your first responsibility is to your audience, who will expect good organization and delivery of materials. Practise your planned presentation with a live audience, coach, or video camera.

CHECKLIST FOR ORAL PRESENTATIONS

When preparing presentations, be sure that you have done the following:

- Considered your audience and purpose.
- Done all the research required for the presentation.
- Made an outline of points.
- Written an introduction and a conclusion.
- Practised your presentation with audiovisual support.
- Designed your multimedia presentation with your purpose in mind.
- Selected a suitable design for your multimedia slides.
- Written the text for your slides.
- Illustrated your points with appropriate audio, image, and video files.
- Added appropriate animations and transitions.
- Tested your sequence of slides and edited them ruthlessly.

The following is a brief explanation of some errors commonly found in scientific and technical writing.

ERRORS OF GRAMMAR

Grammar is the structure of an English sentence, called *syntax* by experts in linguistics, and the forms of its words. Each sentence depends for meaning on the order of words and on the form of words, such as the different forms of the verb *drink*: "drink," "drank," and "drunk."

Most writers have some sense of the structure of their first language. This comes from automatic language learning when we are very young. Such learning, a function of the human brain, unfortunately includes errors. At school, we learn about language and develop an understanding of syntax, but this understanding is incomplete and includes errors. Most writers say, "I know what sounds right." This flawed test of grammar is simply applying what we have learned long ago, including the errors.

Fortunately, some errors of syntax are common to most writers. Learn to identify and correct them; seek them out in the final drafts of all your documents.

Sentence Fragment

A sentence fragment is an incomplete sentence, such as "Determining binding constants." An English sentence must have a subject—the person or thing discussed in the sentence—and a predicate—the action or state of being of the subject. A sentence missing one or both of these is a fragment.

Proofread your draft documents carefully, looking for fragments. It seems much easier to spot fragments in someone else's work than in your own. Perhaps a friend can help by reading your report draft for errors.

Run-on Sentence

Many erroneously believe that a run-on sentence is too long. Writing a sentence that contains too many main ideas or strings too many modifiers together is an error of style. The error of grammar called *the run-on sentence* is an error of sentence compounding.

A compound sentence contains two main ideas or principal clauses: "Dogs bark, and cats meow." We usually join principal clauses with a coordinate conjunction: "and," "but," "or," "so," and "yet." However, we can also join principal clauses with a semicolon when the ideas they express are closely related: "Dogs bark; cats meow."

In the *comma splice* form of run-on sentence, the writer has joined principal clauses with a comma: "Dogs bark, cats meow." The comma is only a grammatical pause, marking divisions between subordinate units. Do not use a comma to join principal clauses.

In the *fused* form of run-on sentence, the writer has joined principal clauses with nothing: "Dogs bark cats meow." The lack of a joining word or punctuation makes it difficult for the reader to sort out main ideas within the sentence.

Subject and Predicate Disagreement

Subjects are nouns or pronouns; predicates are verbs or verb phrases. Both nouns and verbs have singular and plural forms; for example, "An external syringe pump circulates the sample" and "External syringe pumps circulate the sample." Note that we add *s* to the noun to make it plural; we add *s* to the verb to make it singular.

Know the correct singular and plural forms of nouns and verbs. If uncertain, check them in a good dictionary.

In each sentence, the subject must agree with its predicate, singular or plural. In the first example above, the singular "pump" agrees with the singular "circulates."

Two factors make a disagreement between the subject and the predicate hard to spot for many writers: long modifying phrases or clauses between the two and sentence subjects that create uncertainty about whether they are singular and plural.

Consider the following sentence with phrase modifiers:

The high stability of such instruments, combined with reference surfaces for detecting nonbinding constants, permit refractive index changes to be measured and account for sample or instrument temperature drifts.

If we extract the bare subject and predicate from the phrase modifiers, we can see the error clearly: "The stability permit changes and account for drifts." The singular subject needs a singular predicate: "The stability permits changes and accounts for drifts."

With its modifiers added back in, the correct sentence reads as follows:

The high stability of such instruments, combined with reference surfaces for detecting nonbinding constants, permits refractive index changes to be measured and accounts for sample or instrument temperature drifts.

Consider the subject of the following sentence:

Every technician and lead hand know the recommended safe procedure.

The words "every" and "each" and their compounds "everyone," "everybody," and so on, are singular in meaning: one of many. Thus the predicate that matches must be singular:

Every technician and lead hand knows the recommended safe procedure.

Pronoun and Antecedent Disagreement

Every pronoun has a noun preceding it somewhere in the text to which the pronoun refers. That noun is called *the antecedent of the pronoun.*

The pronoun must agree with its antecedent in gender, number, and case. Consider the following sentence:

John knew that he had completed the procedure successfully.

The pronoun "he" agrees with the antecedent "John" in gender (both are masculine), number (both are singular), and case ("he" is the subject form of the pronoun required by its use as subject of the subordinate clause "that he had completed the procedure successfully").

Some antecedents refer to people but without gender. Consider the following example:

Everyone carried their own field pack.

The antecedent of the pronoun "their" is "everyone," which is singular in meaning. "Their" is plural and does not agree. The singular pronouns that agree are "his" and "her." Use both; modern style demands inclusive language:

Everyone carried his or her own field pack.

Errors in the Principal Parts of Verbs

Every English verb has three principal parts: the simple present, the simple past, and the past participle. The dictionary lists the simple present (infinitive) form. If no other form is listed, the verb is regular and adds -ed to form the simple past and past participle. If the verb is irregular, the other forms of the verb will be given: "drink," "drank," and "drunk."

Most errors occur in the use of irregular verbs. If you suspect an error in your writing, check the verb's forms in a dictionary. If an error is present, note the correct forms and use them. The following is a list of commonly misused irregular verbs:

Simple Present	Simple Past	Past Participle
drink	drank	drunk
swing	swung	swung
break	broke	broken
freeze	froze	frozen
begin	began	begun
set	set	set
lie	lay	lain
lay	laid	laid

Note the difference between *lie* and *lay*. To lie is to place your body in a horizontal position (we are not concerned here with the regular verb *lie*, meaning to tell an untruth); it is an intransitive verb followed by a predicate noun or adjective: "He has lain asleep for two hours." To lay is to place or put; it is a transitive verb usually followed by a direct object: "I laid my textbook on the computer desk when I had finished."

Misplaced Modifier

Place modifying phrases and clauses close to the words they modify. A reader will associate a modifying element with the words closest to it. If these words are not the intended association, misunderstandings will arise, sometimes in a comical way:

The technician reported that the construction was completed in his e-mail.

The modifier is "in his e-mail." The logical association is with "reported." By placing the modifier at the end of the sentence, the writer associates it with "completed."

Readers can eventually find the correct association by rereading the sentence, but this takes time and causes annoyance. Correct the error in your drafts:

The technician reported in his e-mail that the construction was completed.

Dangling Modifier

Check that your modifiers have a word to modify, usually a noun or a verb. We sometimes lose the intended associations with modifying phrases and clauses in the process of composing sentences.

Having completed the assembly, the instrument calibrated to within 10% of its normal range of values.

The modifying phrase "having completed the assembly" will associate itself in the reader's mind with "the instrument" because it is the closest noun in the sentence. The idea that the instrument completed its assembly by itself is comical. Restore the correct association by adding the noun that belongs with the modifier:

Having completed the assembly, the technician calibrated the instrument to within 10% of its normal range of values.

ERRORS OF PUNCTUATION

Place punctuation marks to identify grammatical units. If you are not sure how to identify grammatical units in a sentence, or which marks are correct, do not punctuate your sentences with inappropriate or incorrect punctuation marks.

Mistakes in punctuation indicate an ignorance of grammar and can seriously mislead the reader as to the meaning of a sentence. Punctuation can completely change the meaning of a sentence:

> The staff says the boss is incompetent.
> The staff, says the boss, is incompetent.

The following are the most commonly used punctuation marks.

Comma

The comma separates grammatical units in a sentence. It is a kind of grammatical pause. Good scientific and technical writing uses short sentences and paragraphs that require fewer commas, but the comma is still the most commonly used and misused punctuation mark.

- *In Compound Sentences*
  Place a comma at the end of each principal clause:

  > The coefficient of friction rose as heat was applied, but thermocouple output remained constant.

- *In Series*
  Separate each pair of items in a list or series with commas:

  > Follow instructions carefully when unpacking the instrument, assembling it, calibrating it for water temperature and dissolved ions, and mounting it in the personal carrier.

- *To Separate Introductory Phrases and Clauses*
  Place a comma after introductory phrases and clauses before the subject of the sentence:

  > After assembling and mounting the instrument, uncoil the cathode lead and trail it in the watercourse behind the unit.

- *To Enclose Nonrestrictive Elements*

Some modifiers are essential to show the reader the complete meaning of the words that they modify. Other modifiers are less essential. They add information about the words they modify, but they are not essential to the meaning of the whole sentence.

We call essential modifying elements restrictive because they restrict the meaning of the words they modify to a specific group. Consider the following:

The college that Mary attends has a linear accelerator.

The restrictive element here is a clause: "that Mary attends." It restricts the word it modifies, "college," to just the one she attends. If we drop the clause, the sentence reads "The college has a linear accelerator," leaving us to wonder which college is meant.

Do not punctuate restrictive elements.

Enclose nonrestrictive elements in commas. Note that you must use two commas. It is a common error to place only one. Consider the following example:

The efficiency of any drill bit, whether used on a cable tool or rotary drill, is compromised by the incorrect use of drilling mud.

The nonrestrictive modifier, "whether used on a cable tool or rotary drill," can be omitted without compromising the sense of the sentence.

Appositives are short, nonrestrictive elements:

Gregory Dudek, a professor of robotics at McGill's Centre for Intelligent Machines, has developed processes for localizing a robot with minimum travel.

- *In Places and Dates*

Many uses of the comma are conventional, that is, we always write a comma in specific situations.

One is place names:

The neutron probe for measuring total moisture content in pavement structures was developed in Airdrie, Alberta, a suburb of Calgary.

Another is dates:

The Confederation Bridge linking Prince Edward Island to the mainland was completed on June 1, 1997, and will be turned over to the Government of Canada in 2032.

Semicolon

Use the semicolon instead of a coordinate conjunction to join principal clauses closely related in meaning:

> This analog test signal is not passed through the smoothing filter of the direct analog converter; instead, the output of the oscillator is connected directly to the multiplexer at the analog-drive converter input.

Note the use in this example of the conjunctive adverb "instead" to link the ideas in the two principal clauses.

Use the semicolon also in some series. When any item in a series contains commas, use the semicolon instead of the comma between the items in the series:

> Do not attempt bioengineering solutions in any of the following situations: severe soil, air, or water contamination; degraded stream bottom; uncontrolled human or animal traffic at the site; or too much shade for selected plant species to thrive.

Colon

Use a colon to introduce a list of additional facts after a complete sentence:

> The Civil Engineering Research Foundation (CERF) identified the following research goals in the architectural industry, in order of importance: computerization, the improvement of design technology and practice, the implementation of computer-integrated design and construction, and the development of new flexible, multiuser design tools.

The colon is a full stop, like the period. Do not place a colon in front of any list in the sentence, as in this example:

> SAW devices include: linear resonator and resonator-filter devices, linear devices using unidirectional IDTs, linear devices using bidirectional IDTs, and nonlinear devices.

The words in this example after "include" are collectively the direct objects of the verb, a natural grammatical relationship. No punctuation is required at all.

ERRORS OF STYLE

Scientific and technical writing describes and explains complex processes, products, and principles. The writer must therefore keep the structure of sentences very simple—single principal clauses with simple subjects and predicates.

The modifying elements in the form of scientific and technical terms will make the sentence longer and more elaborate. Adding complex syntactical structures to complex terminology will obscure meaning even for the most knowledgeable reader.

Keep your style simple and direct. Watch out for the issues described below and simplify whenever possible.

Pronoun References

Pronouns such as "it" or "them" must refer to a specific noun used previously in a sentence or paragraph. This noun is the pronoun's antecedent, and your reader will instinctively look for it. If the correct antecedent is not close to its pronoun, your reader will become confused between possible antecedents or associate the pronoun with the wrong antecedent. Consider the following example:

> After mounting the microbial sensor in the metalworking fluid system, connect the recorder and monitor it.

Does "it" refer to the receiver, the metalworking fluid system, or the microbial sensor? Your reader will not know with any certainty.

Restructure the sentence to make your meaning clear, as in the following example:

1. Mount the microbial sensor in the metalworking fluid system.

2. Connect the recorder.

3. Monitor the recorder output from the sensor for 10 minutes before leaving the installation to ensure the accuracy and stability of both sensor and recorder.

4. Check the recorder every third day and download its memory to a PDA.

Diction

Diction is the choice of words. Choosing the right vocabulary is essential to good scientific and technical writing because of the specialized and often complex terms needed to describe and explain scientific and technical processes and principles.

Use common words. For example, write "He began the investigation" instead of "He inaugurated the investigation."

Parallelism

Make sure that all items in a list have the same grammatical form.

Compounding, also called coordination, is one of two basic structures in an English sentence. The other is subordination. Compounding is joining two or more elements to a sentence using a coordinate conjunction: "and," "but," and "or," along with variations "nor," "either–or," and "neither–nor." We may also include their American cousins "so" and "yet." For example,

The equipment packed for each unit fire crew includes pumps, hoses, stranglers, spare nozzles, and portable radio transceivers.

Write long compounds in the form of a vertical list, usually with bullets:

The equipment packed for each unit fire crew includes the following:
- 2 Wajax pumps, one primary and one backup
- six 100-ft sections of #4 hose
- 2 stranglers
- 2 nozzles, one primary and one spare
- 2 portable radio transceivers.

Note that each item in the bulleted list is a noun with its modifiers, resulting in a parallel construction.

When list items are not parallel, meaning becomes unclear:

This test for desaturase enzyme in plants requires small quantities of plant material, completed in about ten minutes, simple lab equipment and chemicals, and accurate results.

What follows the subject of this sentence is a list that includes verbs, adjectives, and nouns, all different grammatical units. To make the list parallel, make all the items the same unit. For example, use verbs:

This test for desaturase enzyme in plants requires small quantities of plant material, can be completed in about ten minutes, needs only simple lab equipment and chemicals, and produces accurate results.

ERRORS OF USAGE

Writers frequently misuse words in a variety of ways that fall outside the categories of grammar and spelling. Learn the meanings of words by checking them frequently in a good dictionary and by using them in your own sentences.

The following are some common errors of usage.

- *Accept, except.* Do not confuse these. *Accept* means to receive, as in, "The jack for the communications port accepts a standard, 9-pin flat plug." *Except* means to exclude, as in, "The external surface of the robot arm is single-mesh steel except for the alignment sensor mounted on the end to aid its manipulation."
- *Alot.* You wouldn't say "alittle"; don't write "alot." Write "a lot," meaning "many," or use the more formal "a great deal" or "often." The best practice for scientific and technical writers is to omit such vague expressions entirely. Quantify your expressions precisely; for example, "3.5 grams," "512 forest fires," "600 microns," and so on.
- *Amount, number.* This error is now so common that many readers ignore it. However, many do not. *Amount* refers to things you cannot count individually; therefore, you must measure their quantity by weight or volume, as you would with wheat or gasoline. The words associated with amounts are "little–less–least" and "much–more–most." For example, "The amount of medical imaging in Canada will increase as the technology becomes a more digital, distributed process." *Number* refers to things that you can count individually, such as pennies or books. For example, "The number of live cuttings that can be placed in rip rap to improve soil stability depends on rock spacing and the slope of the bank."
- *CD-ROM disk.* CD-ROM stands for "Compact Disk–Read Only Memory." The word *disk* in the expression above is therefore redundant. Omit it. The same is true for *DVD disk*, since DVD means "Digital Video Disk."
- *Data.* The word *data* is the plural of *datum*. Like *criterion–criteria* and *medium–media*, it has Greek origins and does not follow regular English plural forms. Some confusion exists among scientific and technical writers, journalists, and editors regarding whether *data* is plural or singular. The safest choice is plural; for example, "The projected data for atmospheric carbon loadings by 2032 are listed in Table 2."

- *Effect, affect.* Do not confuse these. As a verb, *effect* means "to bring about a change" or "to accomplish," while *affect* means "to influence." For example, "The addition of solvents to the solution effected the desired change in the gram-molecular weight," but "Variations in sample temperature did not affect the accuracy of the study's flow measurements." As nouns, an *effect* is a result, a change produced by an action, as in, "The laser beam in a turbid medium had the effect of scattering photons into ballistic components." *Affect* is a feeling or emotion.

- *If, whether.* The word *if* introduces a condition; for example, "VRML authoring tools have to become more sophisticated if designers are expected to take them as serious development media." *Whether* introduces an alternative, a choice of two options, usually the choice of doing something or not doing it; for example, "Designers have discussed whether to expand the Indexed Line Set to allow VRML models to display different line thicknesses, patterns, or types." Many writers now commonly use *if* as an alternative, as well as a condition, as in this example: "The technical supervisor was uncertain if the new meter would read correctly under field conditions." However, using *whether* for alternatives is clearer for most readers; for example, "The technical supervisor was uncertain whether the new meter would read correctly under field conditions."

- *Principle, principal.* Do not confuse these two. As a noun, *principle* is a rule, natural law, fundamental truth, or guide to behaviour, as in, "The geological principle of superposition says that younger rock strata are higher in the formation." As an adjective, *principal* refers to the leading, the most important person or thing; for example, "The principal means of fire ground attack is the unit crew." As a noun, *principal* can refer to the head of a school or to a sum of money upon which interest is paid. Do not assume that *principal* can refer only to a school principal.

- *Setup, set up.* Many technical writers confuse the noun *setup* with the verb *set up*. The following example shows both used correctly: "Set up the online model with a setup of two-dimensional drawings."

You will find many other mistakes in English usage in both general and technical writing. Make your own lists of correct usage and watch for it in your documents.

SPELLING

Spelling errors can mar the effect of good writing and composition skills. Readers will tend to focus on spelling gaffes and miss the good qualities of your work.

Learn to spell only the words that you need to spell. An active, general interest in words is undoubtedly an asset, but few scientists, engineers, and technicians have this kind of interest in language. It is practical, then, to focus on the words you need to compose clear messages. A good, college-level dictionary of Canadian English is essential to this effort.

The spell checker in your word processing software is a great help in spotting errors. Use it. Microsoft Word comes with a powerful checker that can be set to Canadian English.

Remember that scientific and technical terms are not typically included in the software's list of English words and variations. You will have to add to the word processor's dictionary the terms that you will need when checking your own documents.

Remember also that the spell checker will not find every kind of error. It will find your spelling mistakes and typographical errors quickly and accurately, as long as you have not added incorrect words to its dictionary. However, the spell checker will pass "controls" when you meant "control" or "from" when you meant "to." These "substitution" errors are now common in mass publications that use automated spell checkers. You must proofread drafts of your papers yourself to find these errors and correct them.

Good Spelling Habits

1. Proofread all final drafts of documents for spelling errors. Besides making your writing more correct, this practice identifies for you those words that you typically misspell. List words that you often miss, look them up in a good dictionary, and learn them thoroughly, paying attention to spelling, pronunciation, and various meanings.

2. Learn to pronounce words properly. If you say a word without some of its vowels or consonants, then these omissions will often appear in your written version of the word. Two common examples are "environment" and "government"; if you say "enviroment" or "goverment," then you will likely misspell them.

3. Learn the rules of spelling. Knowing and following some basic conventions is an efficient way to correct spelling because English spellings are, for the most part, consistent. You may have to memorize some individual exceptions to a rule, but learning and following the rule first will help you avoid most mistakes and the waste of time that goes with correcting them or looking up in a dictionary every word you are unsure of. Start with the simple rules given below. Watch for others as you proofread and check your own spelling.

4. Learn the meanings of words. Homonyms, for example, sound the same but are spelled differently and have different meanings, such as "bare" and "bear." The term also applies to words that are similar in sound and spelling but different in meaning, such as "affect" and "effect." Learning word meanings not only helps you spell more correctly but also increases the range, power, and precision of your writing.

Spelling Rules

1. *The* i *before* e *rule.* Many people learned this rule in school as a mnemonic jingle, although some learned only the first part: *i* before *e*, except after *c*, or when sounded as *ay*, as in "neighbour" and "weigh." Apply the rule and you will be correct most times, as in the case of "receive," "conceit," "lenient," and so on. Two exceptions are "weird" and "seize."

2. *Prefixes.* When adding a prefix to a root word, write them together without a hyphen: "un + noticed = unnoticed." Note three common exceptions to this rule, each of which requires a hyphen between prefix and root: (1) root words that begin with capital letters, such as "pre-Mousterian," (2) prefixes that end with a vowel added to root words that begin with a vowel, such as "re-energize," and (3) "self" as a prefix, as in "self-closing doors."

3. *Suffix rule with final silent* e. When a root word ends in a silent *e* and the suffix begins with a consonant, retain the *e* in the root word, as in "hopeful." When a root word ends in a silent *e* and the suffix begins with a vowel, drop the *e* from the root word, as in "hoping."

4. *Suffix rule for doubling final consonants.* When a root word ends in a consonant, double the final consonant when the following three criteria apply: (1) the suffix begins with a vowel, (2) the final single consonant in the root word is preceded by a single vowel, and (3) the root word is accented on the last syllable, as in "occurred" and "beginning." In all other cases, the final consonant remains single, as in "interpreting."

5. *Suffix rule for root words ending in* y. If the *y* is preceded by a consonant, as in "accompany," change the *y* to *i* before adding a suffix, as in "accompaniment," unless the suffix begins with *i*, as in "worrying." If the *y* is preceded by a vowel, as in "annoy," leave the *y* unchanged in front of a suffix, as in "annoying."

6. *Plurals and possessives.* Form regular plurals by adding *s* to the root word: "microchip–microchips," "measurement–measurements," and so on. Plural forms of modern acronyms add *s*: "CDs," "BIOSs," "SMCAs," and so on. Learn irregular plurals as you require them: "mouse–mice," "wolf–wolves," "focus–foci," "criterion–criteria" and so on. Form singular possessives by adding *'s*: "burner–burner's," "switch–switch's," "probe–probe's," and so on. This rule includes words of one syllable that end in *s* or an *s* sound; for example, "Charles's theory" or "Marx's principles of economics." Words of two or more syllables ending in *s* or an *s* sound, add only an apostrophe: "conscience' sake," "Achilles' heel," and so on. Do not use an apostrophe with possessive pronouns: "hers," "his," "its," "ours," and so on. Form plural possessives by adding *s'*: "burners–burners'," "switches–switches'," "probes–probes'," and so on.

Some common words are difficult to spell; memorize them as needed. Below is a partial list of such words:

accommodation	mischief	prejudice	seize
benefit	occurred	privilege	separate
lose	occurrence	receipt	supersede
manoeuvre	parallel	rhythm	

Canadian Spellings

We spell words for historical, not logical, reasons. Time changes language and its spellings. The influence of American English in traditionally British Canada continues to grow in the 21st century. Young people in southern Ontario no longer sit on a chesterfield; they sit on the couch. Where does that leave Canadians?

Work documents in Canada use a blend of British and American spellings. Use this blend for your report. To aid you in this task, make sure that you have and use a college-level dictionary of Canadian English. The following list sets out the main points of the Canadian style of spelling.

- Use British -*re*, not American -*er*, suffixes; for example, "centre" and "theatre," not "center" and "theater." Use British -*our*, not American -*or*, suffixes; for example, "colour" and "humour," not "color" and "humor."
- Use British "cheque," not American "check," when referring to banking.
- Use American -*ize*, not British -*ise* suffixes; for example, "organize" and "itemize," not "organise," "itemise."

APPENDIX B:
BUSINESS ELEMENTS OF
A REPORT

MEMO OR LETTER OF TRANSMITTAL

The purpose of a memo or letter of transmittal is to transmit the report formally to the person or group of people named as the destination on the title page. This business element of a report summarizes the purpose and content of the report, and it transfers responsibility for the report's contents to the reader. Place this element after the title page and before the table of contents. Choose the memo form if the report audience is within your company or agency; choose the letter form if the report audience is outside your company or agency.

Write three paragraphs summarizing the purpose and scope of the study, its methodology and major findings, and your conclusions and recommendations. The last paragraph may also deal with follow-up to the report and list contact information, depending on the workplace situation. See Box B.1 for an example of a memo of transmittal.

MEMORANDUM

To: Prof. C. L. Gulston
From: Jonathan White
Subject: Short-rotation hybrid poplar farming
Date: April 19, 2004

I am pleased to present you with my report on the growth and utilization of poplar in Canada. I am submitting this report in partial fulfillment of the requirements of the Silviculture course in the Forestry Program at Sir Sandford Fleming College.

The following report describes general growth processes in woody stems and then examines these growth processes in poplar. The conclusion emphasizes the opportunities in Canada to take advantage of poplar's wide range, high volume, and fast growth by developing short-rotation poplar farms for veneer, plywood, and pulpwood.

The silvicultural plan set out in this report should stimulate discussion in our course as it has in the poplar industry. I will eagerly await your evaluation of this project. If you have questions, or need further information, please e-mail me at jwhite@flemingc.on.ca or call me at (705) 555–1472.

Box B.1: Memo of Transmittal

EXECUTIVE SUMMARY

An executive summary is longer than an abstract, usually about one page for an average-length report. It covers the methodology, results, and especially conclusions and recommendations in greater detail. Place the executive summary after the other elements of front matter and before the introduction. Some business reports place the executive summary directly in the introduction or at the end of the report after the conclusion. See Box B.2 for an example of an executive summary.

EXECUTIVE SUMMARY

This report presents four main growth processes in woody stems:

• primary growth
• secondary growth
• formation of annual rings
• formation of heartwood and sapwood.

These primary processes determine the utilization of our forest products.

In poplar, primary growth occurs rapidly in root suckers and stump sprouts. Suckers grow faster than seedlings because of their developed root system. Secondary growth produces volume. Canadian poplar sites are similar to European sites that have produced good poplar volume in 4 to 6 years. This short rotation is good for poplar because of the prevalence of decay in mature trees. A rotation age of 30 to 50 years will offset problems of cull. The industry must scale operations for smaller-diameter logs.

The goal of experiments with mini-rotations of poplar is to produce hybrid poplar species with the following characteristics:

• frost-hardiness for northern sites
• high survival rate and growth of root suckers
• good height and diameter growth in root suckers and stump sprouts
• resistance to insects and diseases.

Box B.2: Executive Summary

APPENDIX C:
EMPLOYMENT COMMUNICATIONS

JOB SEARCHING

Today's college graduates and career changers have the choice of multiple career paths. More people are changing jobs and careers in mid-life. Employers demand more from job candidates, so résumés often include two or more postsecondary qualifications in varying fields of study and value-added certificates in specific areas, such as first aid. Most employers now also require solid transferable skills in communications, math, IT, human relations, and more. The Conference Board of Canada reports that employers look for the ability to communicate effectively, to work well with others, and to display initiative.

Most jobs are not made public and must be found by networking or through personal contact directly with employers. Before scanning the job market, reflect on your deepest interests. These may not be the things you do best, but they represent the best long-term choices for your career. Inventory your interests and skills. Research the current job market thoroughly. Remember the following:

- The jobs are there, but they are hidden.
- No single job-searching technique works for every job.
- You have skills and bargaining power with employers.
- The best job seekers, not the most qualified candidates, get the best jobs.

The most effective job search is creative research. Find the companies or agencies that do the type of work you want, based on your assessment of your best skills and favourite field of study. Find the managers with the power to hire you. Approach them directly with your documents.

Use all the research tools at your disposal, including libraries, friends, family, faculty, and the Internet. The best Internet guides to job searching are The Riley Guide and The JobHuntersBible.

Follow these steps in your employment search process:

1. Define your goals.

2. Research employers.

3. Arrange information interviews to deepen your knowledge of the career field in which you want to work.

4. Prepare and send your documents: the employment letter, résumé, and a sample application form.

5. Keep a career portfolio of your achievements and use it.

6. Get employment interviews.

7. Follow up your interviews with appropriate communications.

PORTFOLIOS

A portfolio is a personal collection of documents relating to your work skills and abilities. It is an essential tool in your developing your career. A portfolio represents your potential as an employee; provides depth of information greater than a résumé; documents your knowledge, experience, and achievements; and gives an overview of your employment assets.

To use a portfolio effectively, update its contents regularly as you acquire experience and skills. Select information from the portfolio for your employment letter and résumé that relates to the specific job you are applying for. Review your portfolio before each job interview to keep details fresh in your mind. Make copies of the most relevant portfolio documents and bring them to the interview. In the interview, the portfolio will help you document your success, answer specific questions about your background, and demonstrate your ability to organize information.

A basic career portfolio includes copies of your current résumé and samples of your work. It is recommended that you also include the following:

- a sample letter of application
- letters of reference or recommendation
- thank-you letters to you from employers and volunteer organizations
- certificates, licences, letters of record or academic transcripts

- work-related projects and presentations
- photos of activities and interests.

Include only good, work-related material.

The key to good portfolio design is access to information. Place your documents in a portfolio case with section dividers. Such an arrangement makes it easy to update the portfolio and allows you to arrange documents with the most important and relevant ones at the beginning of each section.

THE LETTER OF EMPLOYMENT

Most employers read the letter of application for employment first. The letter speaks personally to the individual who is reading it, usually someone with the authority to hire you. It is from your letter that this person forms his or her first impression of you; thus, the letter gives you about 30 seconds to make a good first impression that will carry on into the résumé and interview. For this reason, mistakes are costly. The letter is the first step in a screening process. Write and proofread it carefully.

The letter of employment and résumé complement each other. The letter motivates the reader and arouses interest in your application by sketching your best qualifications for the job and specifically requesting an interview. The résumé convinces the reader to give you an interview by providing more detail of your skills and abilities and by offering testimonials in the form of references from people who can confirm your claims.

Keep these goals in mind when writing your letter of employment:

- Make your sentences and paragraphs short. Use a journalistic style and get directly to the point using simple, direct language.
- Communicate facts, not feelings. You may feel hope and fear related to the idea of a good job and meaningful work, but letters do not convey emotion well. You cannot simply claim to be a good employee without proof. Describe your best qualifications in the letter, and let the facts speak for themselves.

The content of your employment letter should follow a natural progression. In the first paragraph, apply for a job. This is a positive beginning to your letter because employers welcome applications. They know that more applications means a greater likelihood of finding good staff. Name the specific job title if you are replying for an advertised position or if you know how the employer labels the job. Indicate where you heard about the job to help the employer determine sources of applicants.

In the second and third paragraphs, sketch your best qualifications. Be specific, factual, and detailed. Devote one paragraph to your best qualification and then a second to another good qualification. If you are a recent graduate, your best qualification is likely your college or university program of study. Another good qualification is a job you've held for a period of time, even if it was part-time or summer employment. The employer likes to see that you have worked.

In the last paragraph, politely request a personal interview at the employer's convenience. Refer the reader to your résumé and provide contact information: your address, phone numbers, fax number, and/or e-mail address.

Use a standard letter format; for details, refer to Chapter 3 of this text. Be neat and accurate. Proofread the letter carefully before sending it. Be objective and factual in describing your achievements. Write no negatives; this is a sales letter. Let the facts speak for you and let the reader draw his or her own conclusions.

THE RÉSUMÉ

The résumé is a fact sheet that highlights your qualifications. It is designed to accompany your employment letter on a separate page. The letter has claims: "Here's what I can do for you." The résumé has credibility: "Here's why you should believe me."

Few résumés get interviews. The employer will usually decide whether to offer an interview within 20 seconds of scanning your résumé. Therefore, the résumé must be well written and designed.

Follow some simple principles of résumé writing:

- Select and arrange information from your portfolio to provide more detail for your strongest qualifications—those related to the job for which you are applying—and to eliminate weak information that doesn't help your application.
- Make your résumé apply to specific market. Use your word processor to tailor your résumé for specific type of work by adding or deleting details.

- Try for one sheet. Most employers prefer it.
- Follow simple principles of résumé formatting:
- Use point-form, left-justified blocks of information.
- Organize top-down, in more-to-less-important order, important being those details most relevant to the position for which you are applying.
- Arrange data under informative headings. Organization impresses an employer and provides quick access to information.
- Enhance headings using capitals or boldface, but keep the typefaces simple.
- Design an attractive, professional format. Space your information well without wasting space.

Résumé Format

The most common formats for résumés are chronological and functional. The chronological résumé lists periods of education and employment by date in reverse chronological order. The functional résumé lists skills and abilities and is recommended here because it emphasizes your experience. A combination or blended résumé summarizes skills and abilities, often called "Highlights of Qualifications," and also lists some important periods of education and employment. The hybrid format is most often recommended for newly graduated college students.

Your résumé should be word processed and printed on good-quality printer, preferably on a laser printer. Special papers can add distinctiveness to your résumé, but some employers actually prefer simple white paper. Use a standard serif or sans serif typeface of 10 to 12 points; fancy typefaces are difficult to read. Use bullets to start each line in your lists of qualifications. Use bolding to enhance headings in the body typeface. Résumés should be one page. Two is also acceptable; three is not.

Résumé Elements

1. *Personal Information*

   - Put your name at the top, enhanced graphically (bold, slightly larger typeface).
   - Include college and permanent addresses in two columns; don't forget home and cell phone numbers and e-mail address.

2. Job Objective

- Be sure to include this section, as it is preferred by employers and gets better results.
- Provide a one-line description of your objective; for example, "An entry-level position as a geological technician in an established company."
- Job objective focuses your résumé and identifies type of work you're looking for. Use multiple résumés and objectives for the different types of work for which you are qualified.
- Describe the position desired in terms of type of work, level of responsibility, location, size and type of company, and so on. Ask yourself what you want to do and where you want to do it.

3. Highlights of Qualifications

- This section is also called "Summary of Qualifications," "Summary," or "Highlights."
- Write three to six short lines of key points about you that can immediately draw the employer's attention.
- Write this section after you have completed your résumé. Be sure that the rest of the résumé supports the claims made in this section with specific details of your work experience and education.
- Focus on highlights such as the following:
  - relevant work experience
  - relevant formal training and education
  - one significant achievement
  - one or two outstanding skills and abilities, such as administrative skills, oral and written communications skills, interpersonal and team skills, or computer skills
  - personal attributes (remember that you must support these claims with facts).

4. Relevant Skills and Experience

- Include relevant skills from all areas of your life, such as work, school, community, and sports and activities.
- Group skills into categories and give them headings; for example, computer skills, technical skills, administrative support, and so on.

- Use one-liners starting with action words, such as "communicated," "assembled," "provided," and so on.
- Make sure that the items listed have parallel grammatical structure.

5. *Employment History*

- List jobs in reverse chronological order.
- Include job title, employer or business name, general location, and dates of employment (month and year).
- Include any volunteer work that fills gaps and gave you skills.

6. *Education*

- List the name of the school, graduation date (year), qualifications (degrees, diplomas, certificates), and any relevant courses.
- Include training here or, if it is extensive, put it in a separate section.

7. *References*

- A reference is someone who agrees to speak to a potential employer about you and your abilities in a positive way. References are usually not listed on your résumé, so put "Available on request" after this heading.
- Employers will ask you for references during an interview. Be prepared with a separate sheet listing references and their contact information.
- Ask your references for permission to use their names before you list them. Remember to thank them for saying nice things about you.
- List four references, including previous employers and personal references. Recent college graduates should always include professors who taught skills relevant to the position sought. Do not include anyone related to you.
- Your references page should have your personal information at the top (see #1 above) and list the details of each references: name, position, company, location, and contact information (phone and fax numbers as well as e-mail address).

John R. Student

College Address	Home Address
34 John St. N.	27 Cowbell Lane
Penticton, BC	Enderby, BC
(604) 555-2281	(604) 555-7620
jstudent@okanagan.bc.ca	jay_599@hotmail.com

Job Objective

An entry-level position as a geotechnical technologist

Highlights of Qualifications

- Good field and technical skills
- Proven ability to work well with others
- Good communications skills

Relevant Skills and Experience

Technical Skills
- Inspected footings for Foothills Hospital (Grady Construction)
- Conducted groundwater studies for Highsite Dam (Mellowell Contractors)
- Analyzed soil engineering data for Hwy 319 (BC Transport)

Supervisory Skills
- Wrote summary report for site investigation (Langdon Mills Engineering)
- Supervised field crew while drilling monitoring wells (Northwest Engineering)
- Trained summer staff for field projects (Northwest Engineering)

Employment History

Field Technologist	Northwest Engineering, Revelstoke	Summer 2007
Technician I	Terra Firm Consulting, Vernon	Summer 2006
Labourer	John Smith Farms, Penticton	Summer 2005

Education

Okanagan Community College, Penticton Campus	2004–2007

- Graduated with Diploma, Geotechnical Technologist

References

Available on request

Box C.1 Sample Student Résumé

APPENDIX D: MICROSOFT WORD XP TUTORIALS

The following tutorials provide brief descriptions of techniques that you can use in Microsoft Word XP to achieve the correct format for specific elements found in most scientific and technical reports. These tutorials are not meant to provide a thorough knowledge of the software, but they can get you started. Keep in mind that the Office Assistant in Word XP can help you with descriptions of menus, commands, and functions.

OUTLINING

The outlining functions in Word XP permit you to move headings and sections and change levels of organization in the hierarchy. The Outline view has powerful features, allowing you to generate a table of contents, format report headings in a variety of styles, restructure an existing document, and so on. Do not confuse these software functions with the creation of an outline of report headings to organize your research notes before you begin to write.

To create a simple outline, refer to Figure D.1 and follow these steps:

1. From the Format menu, select the Bullets and Numbering option. You now have the Bullets and Numbering menu open in a separate window.

2. Select the Outline Numbered tab on the top of the Bullets and Numbering menu. You may now select the style of numbering you wish for your outline. Do not choose a style that contains the word "Heading." Complete the command by clicking OK at the bottom of the window.

3. If you wish to customize the numbering system for your outline, select the Customize button at the bottom of the Bullets and Numbering menu. You now have the Customize Outline Numbered List menu from which you may select your own outline number format, style, and position for each level of organization (see Figure D.2).

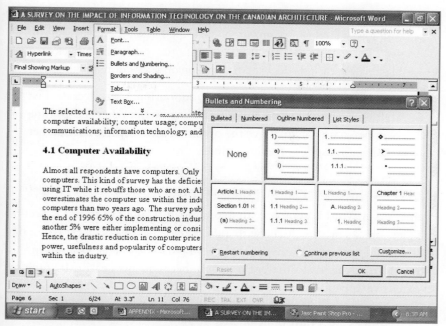

Figure D.1: Format Menu with Bullets and Numbering

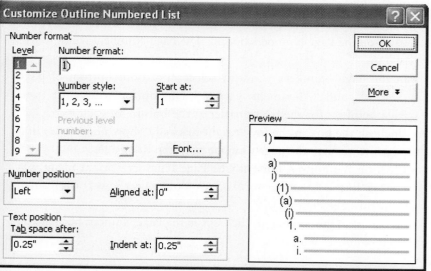

Figure D.2: Customize Outline Numbered List Menu

4. Enter your text for each heading in your outline. To shift a heading to a lower level of organization, click the Decrease Indent icon on your Formatting toolbar. If you wish to move a heading back to a higher level, click the Increase Indent icon on your Formatting toolbar.

5. An alternate method of formatting your outline is to select the List Styles tab on the Bullets and Numbering menu. As in the Outline Numbered menu, you have the option of customizing the number and heading styles of your outline.

INSERTING PAGE NUMBERS

Pagination in Word is complex. To avoid the difficulties of inserting section and page breaks in a single file with all report elements, create two files: one for the front matter and another for the report body. This separation will allow you to create two different page number sequences easily. If you have an extensive appendix, create a third file for it.

Page Numbers for Front Matter

Put in one file all the elements of the front matter that your report requires, from the title page to the abstract. Make sure they are in the correct order (for details, see Chapter 3).

- To insert page numbers, go to the Insert menu.
- Click on the Page Numbers option. The Page Numbers window will pop up.
- In the Page Numbers window, select "Position: Bottom of page (Footer)" and "Alignment: Center." This option will centre your page numbers for the front matter at the bottom of each page.
- Uncheck the box in the lower right marked "Show number on first page" to remove the page number from the title page.
- Click on the Format button. The Page Number Format menu will appear. In the "Number format" window, select lowercase Roman numerals. See Figure D.3.
- To complete the command, click OK in the Page Number Format and Page Numbers windows.

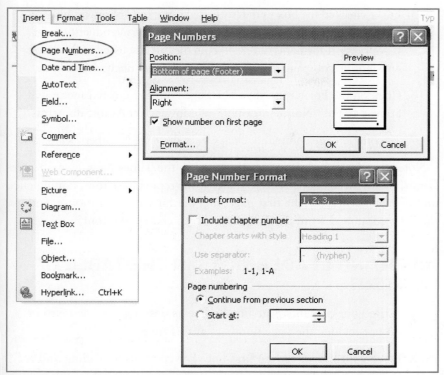

Figure D.3: Page Numbering Menus

Page Numbers for Report Body

1. Put in one file all the elements of the body that your report requires, from the introduction to the list of references page. Make sure they are in the correct order.

2. To insert page numbers, go to the Insert menu.

3. Click on the Page Numbers option. The Page Numbers window will pop up.

4. In the Page Numbers window, select "Position: Top of page (Header)" and "Alignment: Right." This option will place your page numbers for the body in the top right corner of each page.

5. Leave checked the box in the lower right marked "Show number on first page" to start the page numbering from the introduction page. If your report format is different from the one discussed in this book and requires no page number on the first page, uncheck the box.

6. Click on the Format button. The Page Number Format menu will appear. In the "Number format" window, select Arabic numerals.

7. To complete the command, click OK in the Page Numbers window.

Note that the default page numbers are in the Times New Roman typeface. If you wish to change this to match your report base font, double-click on the page number on the first page, highlight it with your mouse, and use the Font command from the Format menu to change the font.

INSERTING LEADER DOTS IN THE TABLE OF CONTENTS

1. Write your contents page line by line as described in the text but do not include the page numbers at this time.

2. Place your cursor on the first line that contains a heading and a page number. Be sure your Ruler is showing. (If it is not, select it from the View menu.)

3. Before you can insert leader dots between the heading to the page number, you must first set the correct tab stop where you wish to place your page number column. Go to the Format menu and select the Tabs command.

4. In the Tabs window, type in the value for the tab stop position where you want the page numbers to appear (see Figure D.4). This value can be estimated by looking at the Ruler.

5. Select "Right" from among the "Alignment" options. Remember that the page number column must be on the right side of the contents page.

6. To insert leader dots from the heading to the page number, select item 2 under "Leader." This style of leader dots is the standard used in technical reports. Click OK to set the command.

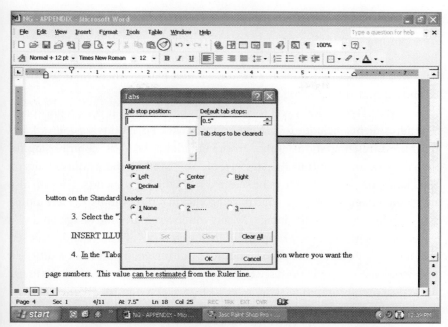

Figure D.4: Tabs Menu and Format Painter Icon

7. To insert leader dots on the line, begin with your cursor at the end of the heading on the first line. Hit the Tab key. The cursor will move to the special tab position and insert leader dots. Type the page number. Repeat for each new line.

8. If you need to insert leader dots and page numbers in lines with headings already typed, use the Format Painter command. Activate Format Painter with the brush icon, the location of which is circled in Figure D.4. With your cursor placed on the line that already contains the special tab and leader dots, double-click on the brush icon. Doing this identifies the line that contains the formatting you want to replicate elsewhere in the document. Move your cursor to the line where you want to have the special tab and leader dots. Notice that the cursor has changed to a brush icon. Left click to place the leader dots. Repeat this for as many lines as needed. When you are finished, click the cursor on the brush icon again to turn it off.

188 Appendix D

WRAPPING TEXT AROUND FIGURES

You can bring graphics into a Word file with the Picture command in the Insert menu. You can also directly copy images from other software, such as a web browser or Adobe Illustrator, by first placing them on a Windows clipboard and then pasting them into Word.

Microsoft Word allows you to adjust a graphic image on your report page. The adjustments include greyscaling or watermarking, modifying contrast and brightness, resizing and rotating, cropping, adding borders, compressing for web display, and customizing page layout. You can find these adjustments on the Picture toolbar (which can be selected from the View menu). You can also move the image around on your page by clicking and holding the left mouse button while you drag the image. When you insert a graphic image on a text page, the image appears wrapped "in line with text." This is the default setting and may be a suitable page layout for your image. If you want a different text-wrapping style, you must select another wrapping mode. To select an image and select a text-wrapping style, refer to Figure D.5 and follow these steps:

1. Select your image by left clicking on it. Little square "handlebars" will appear along the edges of the image. These allow you to resize the image by clicking and dragging.

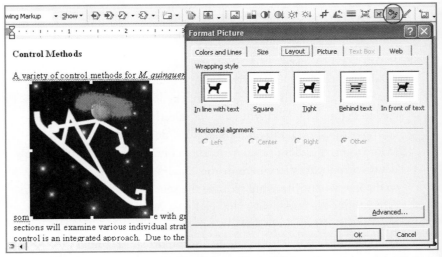

Figure D.5: Selected Pictures with Handlebars, Circled Picture Format Icon, and Picture Format Menu

NEL

2. After you select the image, notice the Format Picture icons on the toolbar. Note that you can also right click the image to produce an instant menu from which you can select the Format Picture commands.

3. Click on the Format Picture icon on the Format Picture toolbar (the circled icon in Figure D.5). This will bring up the Format Picture menu in a new window.

4. In the Format Picture window, left click on the Layout tab.

5. Choose from the wrapping styles shown by left clicking on the appropriate icon. Four of the five options also allow you to select the horizontal alignment of your graphic image on the text page.

6. The Advanced button on the Format Picture menu will bring up the Advanced Layout options in a new window. These controls let you adjust the text wrapping and the position of your image more exactly (see Figure D.6).

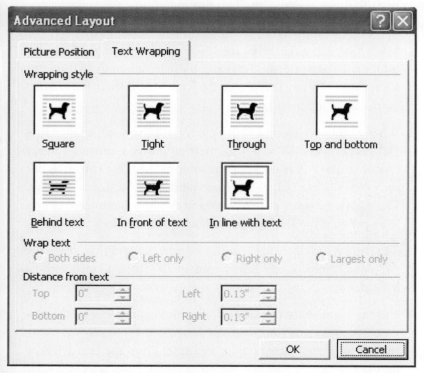

Figure D.6: Advanced Layout Menu

For large images, the "Top and bottom" layout is best. Give your images room on the page. For smaller images, use "Square" or Tight" layout. The Advanced Layout controls allow you to increase the distance of the image above and below your report text. Experiment with your image and text to get the right amount of white space around your image.

FIGURE NUMBER AND TITLE FOR SMALL FIGURES

For a large image with the "Top and bottom" layout, place the required figure number and title below the figure using regular text. For a small image using the "Square" or Tight" layout, insert the required figure number and title with the Text Box function as described below.

A Text Box is actually a graphic image that contains text. Treat it as you would treat an image, including using its handles to resize it and text wrap to arrange text around it. Within the box, choose the same font as in your report text. To do so, selecting the Text Box and choose the appropriate style and size of font in the Formatting toolbar.

1. Select Text Box either from the Insert menu or from the Drawing toolbar. To activate the Drawing toolbar, selecting it from the View menu. Figure D.7 shows the icon for the Text Box circled on the Drawing toolbar.

2. When you have selected Text Box, your cursor will change to a "+" shape. Word XP will also insert a "drawing canvas," a grey box that says, "Create your drawing here." This canvas is for drawing multiple shapes that you can move or resize as a group. The drawing canvas is unnecessary in this application, so remove it by pressing the Delete key on your keyboard.

3. To create a Text Box for your figure number and title, place the "+" cursor immediately below your small image, aligned with its left side.

4. Use the handlebars on the new Text Box to resize it into a rectangle the width of your image and high enough to accommodate the text of your figure number and title. From the font window on the Formatting toolbar (circled in Figure D.8), select the style and size of your report base font. Type an appropriate figure

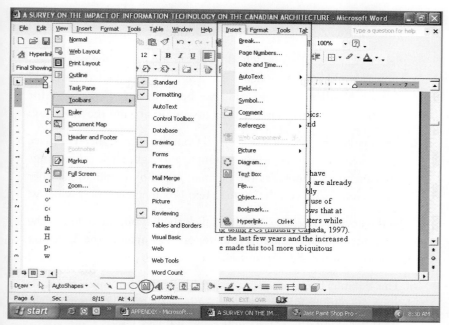

Figure D.7: View and Insert Menus

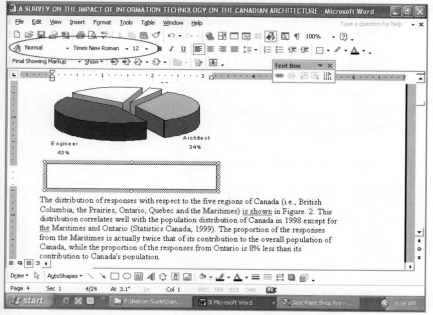

Figure D.8: Text Box Formation

number and title for your image. Add an appropriate citation if you borrowed the graphic from a secondary source.

5. Select your Text Box by left clicking on it; the outline of the rectangle should be surrounded with hachures (light, angled lines) and contain handlebars for resizing the box. Refer to Figure D.9 for the following steps to make your text wrap around the Text Box.

6. Select either the Text Box command from the Format menu or place your cursor on the Text Box rectangle and right click. This brings up a menu that includes the Format Text Box command. Either selection will give you the Format Text Box menu in a new window.

7. In the Format Text Box window, click the Layout tab. Choose the same method of wrapping your report text around the Text Box as you used for the figure itself.

8. The default Text Box has a solid black line outlining the text. Such an outline is not appropriate in a report. To eliminate the solid line, click the Colors and Lines tab (see Figure D.9).

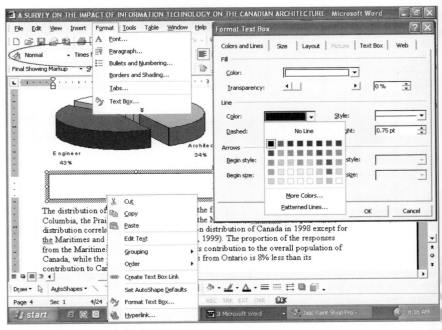

Figure D.9: Text Box Selection

9. In the "Line" area, click the down arrow on the right side of the "Color" rectangle. The colour palette will appear.

10. Choose "No Line" option above the palette. This option gets rid of Text Box outline. Click OK to execute the command. Note that you can still click on the Text Box after you have eliminated the outline.

HANGING INDENTATION FOR REFERENCE LISTS

Format reference lists using hanging indentation. This setup makes it easier for your reader to see surnames. The first line of each entry begins on the left margin; the second and successive lines begin about five spaces from the left margin.

Microsoft Word XP considers each entry in your list to be a paragraph. The default paragraph format begins on the default left margin of your page. In order to change this format to hanging indentation for your reference list entries, follow these steps:

1. Click your cursor anywhere in the first entry of your reference list. The paragraph format command applies only to the paragraph where your flashing cursor is located when you activate the command.

2. Select the Paragraph option from the Format menu. This will bring up the Paragraph menu in a separate window.

3. Choose the "Indents and Spacing" tab (see Figure D.10). In the "Indentation" area of the window, click the down arrow on the right side of the rectangle under the "Special" window.

4. Select "Hanging." If you have your line spacing set to "Double" as required in the body of your report, change this now to "Single" if your type of reference list requires it. Click OK to execute the command.

5. Use the Format Painter (see Figure D.4) to transfer the hanging indentation format from the paragraph you just formatted to the other entries in your list.

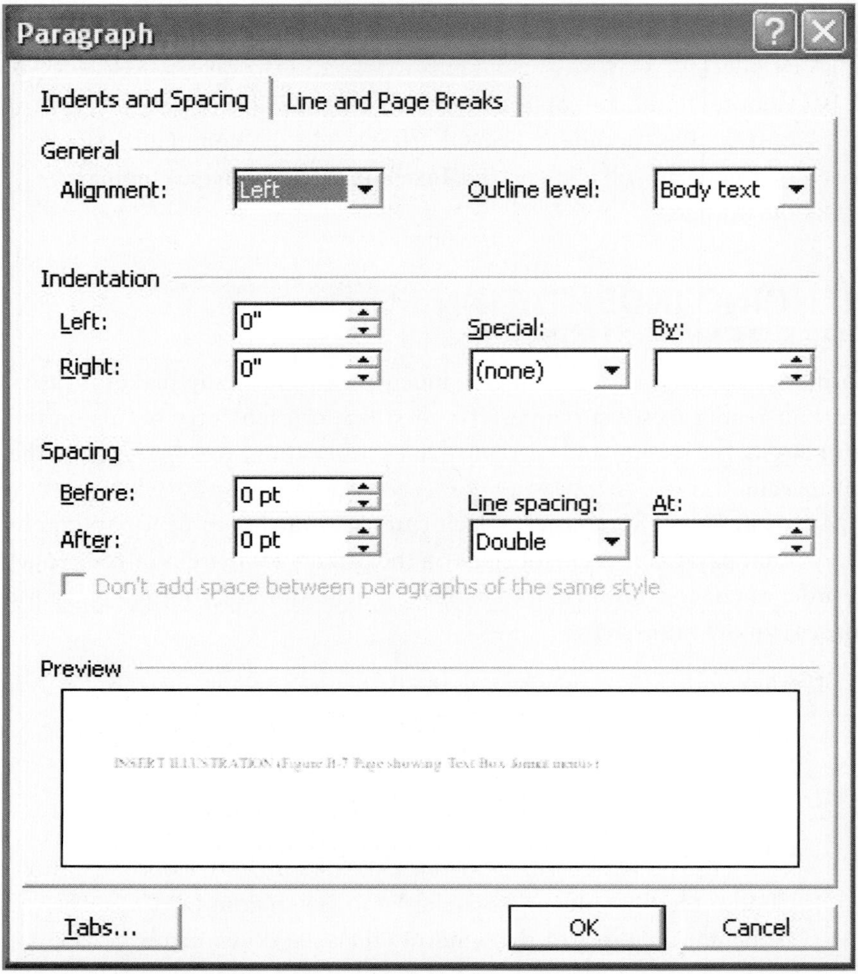

Paragraph [?] [X]

Indents and Spacing | Line and Page Breaks

General
Alignment: [Left ▼]   Outline level: [Body text ▼]

Indentation
Left: [0"] ↕   Special: [(none) ▼]   By: [ ] ↕
Right: [0"] ↕

Spacing
Before: [0 pt] ↕   Line spacing: [Double ▼]   At: [ ] ↕
After: [0 pt] ↕

☐ Don't add space between paragraphs of the same style

Preview

    INSERT ILLUSTRATION (Figure II-7 Page showing Text Box format menus)

[Tabs...]   [OK]   [Cancel]

Figure D.10: Paragraph Menu

INSERTING MATHEMATICAL EQUATIONS

Insert mathematical equations into your Word document using Microsoft Equation Editor 3.0. You must first install this feature of Microsoft Office XP on your computer. Refer to Figure D.11 as you follow these steps:

1. Place the cursor at the location where you want to insert a mathematical equation.

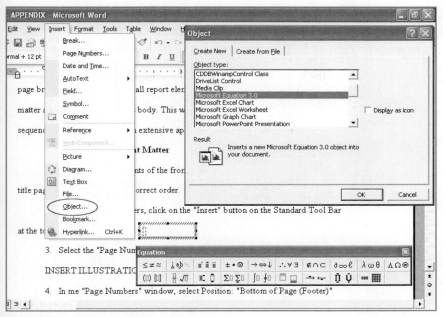

Figure D.11: Object and Equation Menus

2. From the Insert menu, select Object. This gives you the Object window, from which you can select Microsoft Equation 3.0 by highlighting it and clicking the OK button.

3. You now have the equation object box, which looks much like a Text Box, in your text and the Equation menu as a window floating above your text. Notice that the flashing cursor appears in the equation object box within a rectangle defined by a dotted line. The symbols and numerical values that you insert will appear within the rectangle.

4. Insert mathematical symbols by selecting them from the Equation menu. Insert numbers and other characters directly from the keyboard. Select, move, resize, and text-wrap the equation object box just like the Text Box to suit your page requirements.

APPENDIX E:
SAMPLE STUDENT REPORT

Note: The following sample report is intended only as a model of correct report format as set out in this text, using the CSE name-year style of documentation.

**THE STRUCTURE AND GROWTH OF TREE STEMS
AND THEIR IMPORTANCE TO THE GROWTH AND UTILIZATION
OF POPLAR (*POPULUS*) IN CANADA**

By
Jonathan White

To
Professor C. L. Gulston

March 23, 2007

TABLE OF CONTENTS

Page

ii

LIST OF ILLUSTRATIONS

Page

ABSTRACT

Primary growth and secondary growth of stems are the two most important processes that contribute to the total growth of trees. They are the major determining factors of utilization of our forest products. Primary growth is responsible for tree height, while secondary growth produces greater diameter.

This paper outlines briefly the main structures of woody stems and describes the processes determining their growth. It relates these processes to the utilization of poplar (*Populus*) in Canada. It identifies conditions that limit mature stem growth and summarizes research into improvement of stem growth and management of environmental factors affecting poplar silviculture.

iv

1

INTRODUCTION

Purpose and Scope

The purpose of this report is to describe the growth processes of woody stems in simple terms to provide a framework for discussing the growth characteristics of poplar (*Populus*) in Canada with a view to applying these to poplar management. These data are a summary of well-established processes of tree physiology and current research into short-rotation poplar management.

The following are the four main growth processes presented in this report: primary growth, secondary growth, annual rings, and the formation of heartwood and sapwood. This report then examines these processes in poplar (*Populus*) species in Canada, including large- and small-toothed aspen, cottonwood, and European hybrid species.

The poplar section of the report describes primary and secondary growth processes in poplar species and factors affecting each type of growth. It ends with a discussion of short-rotation poplar stands that take advantage of fast growth and minimize the effect of pests and disease in mature stands.

2

Review of Literature

Any secondary school or postsecondary school textbook of botany, plant physiology, or plant growth is suitable for gaining insight into the primary and secondary growth of stems. However, a particularly useful source quoted throughout this paper is *Botany of woody stems* by Luger and Jarrell, 2001.

A good summary of the growth and utilization of poplar is the proceedings of a poplar symposium that took place in Cornwall, Ontario, and Syracuse, New York, in 1987 at a joint meeting of the Poplar Councils of Canada and the United States. The publication, edited by Fayle et al. (1979) is entitled *Poplar research, management and utilization in Canada*.

For a complete review of the literature, see Palmer's *Short-rotation culture of populus and larix: a literature review* (1991).

3

TREE GROWTH PROCESSES

Primary Growth in Stems

The stem is the structure, usually above the ground, which bears the leaves and branches of the tree (Shigo, 1994:53). Stems vary greatly in structure; each species differs in the way it combines cells into complex systems based on the vascular tissues that bind the stem together, conduct moisture, and give it strength.

Structures

Growth in trees occurs only in specific tissues called meristems or meristematic tissue. In the meristematic tissue, under favourable conditions, new cells are continually being formed as some or all of the cells repeatedly divide (Browse, 1988:401). The most important meristems in the tree are the apical-stem meristem and the vascular cambium, respectively related to primary and secondary growth (Browse, 1988:401).

4

Growth Sequence

There are three regions or zones in the apical stem, or tip of the terminal bud of the tree, which all play their parts during primary growth, or
growth in stem length.

The region at the very tip of the stem, the first $1/4$ inch, is the meristematic area (see Figure 1). The leaf primordium protects this area of
active cell division or mitosis. Below this area is the zone of cell elonga-
tion, the only area where upward growth takes place (Luger and Jarrell,
2001:126). In this zone, the undifferentiated parenchyma cells absorb
water and cause the cells to enlarge vertically. The lowest is the zone of
cell maturation where the now specialized or differentiated parenchyma
cells begin to form the primary tissues: xylem, phloem, and cambium.
The entire process could be visualized as a stalagmite growing on the
floor of a cave. Throughout the entire process of primary growth, the
apical-stem meristematic tissue is continually producing new cells
(Luger and Jarrell, 2001:128).

5

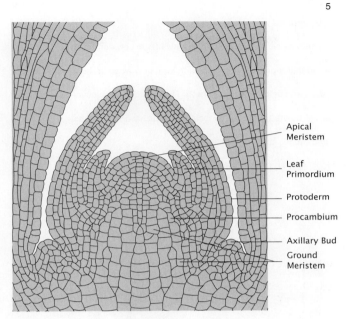

Apical
Meristem

Leaf
Primordium

Protoderm

Procambium

Axillary Bud

Ground
Meristem

Figure 1. Regions of apical meristem (Luger and Jarrell, 2001: 253)

Secondary Growth in Stems

This results from the activity of the vascular cambium, which is also a

form of meristematic tissue, and is characterized by an increase in stem

thickness or diameter.

6

Structures

The cork cambium is a one-cell-thick layer between the bark and wood that repeatedly subdivides to form new wood and bark cells, or xylem and phloem (see Figure 2). The cork cambium usually becomes active before the primary vascular tissues have become fully differentiated (Luger and Jarrell, 2001: 132).

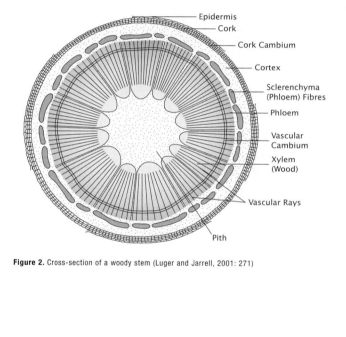

Figure 2. Cross-section of a woody stem (Luger and Jarrell, 2001: 271)

7

Growth Sequence

The cambium cells divide and produce primary xylem on the inner side and primary phloem on the outer side (see Figure 3) within the vascular bundles. They then lay down secondary xylem on the inner side of the primary xylem and secondary phloem on the inner side of the primary phloem (Luger and Jarrell, 2001: 139).

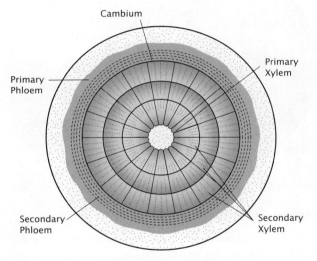

Figure 3. Primary and secondary growth cells (Luger and Jarrell, 2001: 152)

8

Annual Rings

By the end of the first growing season, the stem has its first annual
growth ring (see Figure 4). This consists of a small amount of primary
phloem next to the pith, the remainder of the ring being secondary xylem.

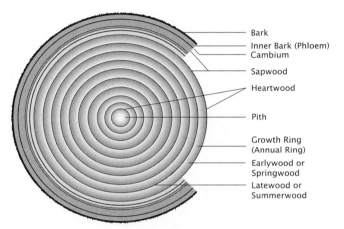

- Bark
- Inner Bark (Phloem)
- Cambium
- Sapwood
- Heartwood
- Pith
- Growth Ring (Annual Ring)
- Earlywood or Springwood
- Latewood or Summerwood

Figure 4. Formation of annual growth rings (Shigo, 1994: 24)

Primary and Secondary Xylem and Phloem

The cambium forms secondary xylem and secondary phloem year after
year during the life of the tree (Luger and Jarrell, 2001: 164). The pressure

9

of new tissue formed within the ring gradually crushes the older phloem cells but not the secondary xylem cells that eventually form the bulk of the stem. The compression of phloem cells also happens because of the faster rate of production of xylem cells, 75 to 100 times as fast (Luger and Jarrell, 2001: 165).

Springwood and Summerwood

Each annual ring contains springwood and summerwood (see Figure 4). Springwood is that portion of the annual growth ring formed during the early part of the growing season. In the spring, when growth is fast, the primary growth cells are larger and thinner-walled than those produced in the summer. These cells carry water for developing leaves, shoots, and flowers (Luger and Jarrell, 2001: 165).

The number and size of summerwood cells exceed those of springwood because the summer growing season is longer than that of spring. The width of each annual ring reveals the environmental influences on a tree's growth for that year. Cooler, more moist conditions produce wider rings.

10

Formation of Heartwood and Sapwood

Conversion of sapwood into heartwood as xylem tissue increases in age is the result of changes in colour, composition, and structure of various elements. Sapwood is the living wood of pale colour near the outside of the stem and is susceptible to decay. Sapwood cells carry oxygen and mineral sap up the tree (Browse, 1988: 132). The inner portion of the sapwood turns into heartwood as the tree ages.

As sapwood ripens into heartwood, the walls of any remaining living cells of xylem increasingly lignify, that is, harden to preserve cellulose. After they lignify, the xylem cells die. They lose their water content; oils, resins, tannins, and gums accumulate (Browse, 1988: 133). These latter materials make heartwood darker and more decay-resistant than sapwood. Heartwood is the wood extending from the pith, the soft-centred core of the tree, to the sapwood. Heartwood cells no longer participate in the life processes of the tree; however, they strengthen the tree and make it rigid if not exposed to air.

The radius of the heartwood increases with the age of the tree whereas that of the sapwood remains approximately the same (Browse, 1988: 134).

GROWTH PROCESSES IN POPLAR

Poplar as a Resource

Poplars are widely distributed throughout the northern hemisphere, chiefly in the temperate zone. They are fast growing, short-lived trees. The wood is light and soft; it has inconspicuous growth rings. It is used for veneer, plywood, lumber, boxes, small woodenware, and barrels for dry goods. As a pulpwood species, poplar ranks high among the hardwood species, and it is also the main resource for the fibreboard and particleboard industry (Farrar, 1995: 118).

Poplars have the widest range and greatest volume of any of the hardwood genera, yet only an insignificant part of the theoretical yield is harvested and utilized. In Europe and Asia, the genus has received much scientific study and has been intensively cultivated in many countries over a wide range of growing conditions for many years (Pfeiffer, 1978: 2).

In Canada, the general trend toward a greater utilization of hardwood species, together with reduced wood supplies in areas close to mills, is focussing attention on species such as poplar that have a capacity for high yields on short rotations (Pfeiffer, 1978: 2).

12

Primary Growth

Importance to Vegetative Reproduction

Plantations of either native or hybrid species take advantage of primary growth characteristics of poplar by utilizing vegetative reproduction. Most poplar species propagate chiefly by means of suckers, or new stems, that arise from roots near the surface of the ground, a characteristic of great importance in regenerating poplar on cut-over or burned-over areas (Farrar, 1995: 118).

Another method of asexual or vegetative reproduction is stump and collar sprouts. If a stem is cut and part of the stump or root collar is left in the ground, new shoots will again appear. Depending on when the stems are cut, this process can happen more than once in the same growing season (Barkley, 1983: 3).

Factors Affecting Primary Growth

Poplar suckers originate singly or in clumps; the height of dominant shoots in a clump increase with an increase in the number of shoots per clump. Height growth of trembling aspen (*Populus tremuloides*) suckers

13

is initially faster than that of seedlings because of their already well-developed root system (Pfeiffer, 1978: 2).

Poplars have high moisture content. The average moisture content of trembling aspen in winter decreases in summer months. Since height growth occurs only in the apical meristem by the absorption of water and the moisture content of poplar is high, the best primary growth will take place on a moist site. For initial establishment of native and hybrid poplar species, sufficient moisture combined with well-aerated soil are basic requirements (Barkley, 1983: 8).

Secondary Growth

Secondary growth in poplar produces diameter faster as primary growth slows.

Factors Affecting Secondary Growth

A short rotation age is desirable because poplar is prone to decay as the trees get older (Armson and Smith, 1978: 21). A rotation age of between 30 and 50 years would offset this problem. However,

14

poplar-based industries then have to make greater use of small logs if the problem of decay is to be overcome (Fayle et al., 1979: 19).

Insects and diseases that attack the stem are also a limiting factor on utilization of poplar and affect the quality of secondary growth. Some examples of these are borers, heart rot, cankers, and galls. Various species attack the xylem, cambium, phloem, and sapwood regions of the stem (Barkley, 1983: 29). Together, insects and diseases cause great differences between gross stand volume estimates and actual net merchantable volume.

Short Rotation Yields

Poplar has the capacity for high yields on short rotations (Pfeiffer, 1978: 26). Since yield is measured in units of volume, poplar producers look for acceptable diameter growth in a short period. Processing machinery for pulp and paper, particleboard, and fibreboard industries is specific for specific sizes of logs.

15

CONCLUSION

Summary

There are two major processes involved in the growth of stems in trees: primary and secondary growth, which result in the formation of annual rings and heartwood and sapwood in the tree with its increasing maturity.

Primary growth is responsible for growth in height whereas secondary growth causes an increase in diameter. Both these processes result in an increase in volume and thus potential merchantable value. Terminal growth is usually completed in the early part of the growing season, but lateral growth continues sometimes until frost. Primary tissues make up a relatively small amount of volume, and after secondary growth has proceeded for some time, these tissues play an insignificant role in the life of the tree.

With respect to poplar (*Populus*), primary growth is rapid in the various forms of vegetative reproduction: root suckering and stump sprouts. Sufficient moisture and well-aerated soil are two conditions that promote primary growth.

16

Secondary growth in poplar may produce adequate volumes for pulp-wood and other uses on a short-rotation basis. Hybrid species are able to supply this volume successfully, although adapting existing processing machinery to small-diameter logs is an economic barrier. Because poplar is prone to decay and attacks from insects and disease with increasing age, good diameter growth in a short time period is doubly important.

Discussion

Mini-rotations

In the search to develop fast-growing trees with good-quality wood, federal and provincial research centres have crossed native and European species of poplar to produce hybrids with the following characteristics:

- frost-hardiness to utilize northern sites
- high survival rate and growth of root suckers
- good height and diameter growth in stump sprouts

These mini-rotation experiments to improve volume complement

17

other experiments to develop a poplar crop that will be resistant to many

diseases and insects. The new Ontario poplar clones (Anonymous,

1984) will increase the net merchantable volume and solve the problem

of high cull rates.

Short-rotation Biomass Production

In eastern Ontario, for instance, hybrid poplar clones are producing

annual dried biomass comparable to field crops (Pfeiffer, 1978: 4).

Hybrid poplar for pulp yields biomass amounts similar to native poplar;

however, it has slightly different physical properties that require chem-

ical and physical adjustments in the pulping process (see Table 1).

Table 1. Pulp yields for hybrid poplar, native poplar, and mixed hardwoods
(% harvested wood) (Pfeiffer, 1978: 5)

Wood Tested	Magnefite Pulps		Kraft Pulps	
	Unbleached	Bleached	Unbleached	Bleached
Hybrid cottonwood (a)	50.2	47.3	49.7	47.8
Hybrid cottonwood (b)	50.1	47.2	50.2	48.3
Hybrid aspen	51.9	49.6	51.3	49.6
Regular mill poplar	53.7	50.7	55.4	53.6
Dense mixed hardwoods	47.5	43.9	46.9	45.3

18

Experiments with hybrid poplar as a livestock feed suggest that ruminants can digest *in vitro* up to 47% of aspen species of poplar with appropriate treatment of the wood. Treated woods can contribute to dietary energy and roughage needs of ruminants. Using hybrid poplar as fuel is more problematic. Burning wood is inefficient and polluting. However, wood will produce methanol to blend with petroleum as a source of fuel (Pfeiffer, 1978: 5–18).

The aim is a continuous production on a yearly basis of adequate volume to meet demands for veneer, plywood, lumber, particleboard, and fibreboard, as our supplies of conifers diminish or become too expensive to harvest. This objective has been successful in some areas of Canada. As better hybrids and poplar management strategies develop, poplar farming will continue be a part of the Canadian forest industry.

19

LIST OF REFERENCES

Anderson HW, Zsuffa L. 1975. Yield and wood quality of hybrid cottonwood grown in two-year rotation In Economic potentials of
hybrid poplar-based fibre production as an agricultural enterprise in eastern Ontario. Pfeiffer, WC. 1978. Toronto: Ontario
Ministry of Natural Resources. 68 p.

[Anonymous]. 1983. Methods of rapid, early selection of poplar clones for
maximum yield potential: a manual of procedures. St. Paul,
MN.: North Central Forest Experiment Station, Forest Service,
U.S. Dept. of Agriculture. 43 p.

[Anonymous]. 1984. A guide to the identification of poplar clones in
Ontario. Maple, ON: Ontario Tree Improvement and Forest
Biomass Institute, Ontario Ministry of Natural
Resources. 34 p.

[Anonymous]. 2003. The preservation of wood: a self-study manual for
wood treaters. Communication and Educational Technology
Services, University of Minnesota Extension Service. [Online].
Available from: http://www.extension.umn.edu/distribution/
naturalresources/components/6413ch1.html. Accessed 2003
Sept 27.

Armson KA, Smith JHG. 1978. Management of hybrid poplar. Case
study 5, in forest management in Canada. Ottawa: Canadian
Forestry Service FMR-X-103. 27 p.

Barkley BA. 1983. A silvicultural guide for hybrid poplar in Ontario.
Toronto: Ontario Ministry of Natural Resources. 17 p.

Browse PM. 1988. Plant propagation. New York: Simon &
Schuster. 254 p.

20

Bryce J, Temler J. 1974. Evaluation of one and two-year-old hybrid poplar. *In* Economic potentials of hybrid poplar-based fibre production as an agricultural enterprise in eastern Ontario. Pfeiffer, WC. 1978. Toronto: Ontario Ministry of Natural Resources. 68 p.

Dirr M. 1987. The reference manual of woody plant propagation: from seed to tissue culture. Athens, GA: Varsity Press. 53 p.

Farrar, JL. 1995. Trees in Canada. Markham, ON: Fitzhenry & Whiteside and Canadian Forest Service, Natural Resources Canada, in cooperation with the Canada Communication Group Publishing, Supply and Services Canada. 268 p.

Fayle DCF, Zsuffa L, Anderson HW, editors. 1979. Poplar research, management and utilization in Canada. Proceedings of the North American Poplar Council Annual Meeting. Brockville, Ontario. 1977 Sep 6–9. Toronto: Ontario Ministry of Natural Resources. 84 p.

Hoadley RB. 1990. Identifying wood: accurate results with simple tools. Newtown, CT: The Taunton Press. 264 p.

Johnson H. 1973. The international book of trees. New York: Simon & Schuster. 429 p.

Krempels D. 2003. Plant organs: root, stem and leaf. [Online]. University of Miami Faculty of Biology. Available from: http://fig.cox.miami.edu/Faculty/Dana/105F00_8. Accessed 3 Oct 2003.

Luger JH, Jarrell, RH. 2001. Botany of woody stems. Boston: Sevier. 153 p.

Maini JS, Cayford JH, ed. 1968. Growth and utilization of poplar in Canada. Canada Department of Forestry and Rural Development. Publication No. 1205: 116–144. 76 p.

Macdonald B. 1986. Practical woody plant propagation for nursery growers. Portland, OR: Timber Press. 66 p.

21

More D, White J. 2002. The illustrated encyclopedia of trees. Portland, OR: Timber Press. 237 p.

Palmer CL. 1991. Short-rotation culture of populus and larix: a literature review. Sault Ste. Marie, ON: Canada-Ontario Forest Resource Development Agreement. 55 p.

Pfeiffer WC. 1978. Economic potentials of hybrid poplar-based fibre production as an agricultural enterprise in eastern Ontario. Toronto: Ontario Ministry of Natural Resources. 36 p.

Shigo AL. 1994. Tree anatomy. Durham, NH: Shigo and Trees, Associates. 361 p.

INDEX